"This book is a blessing that gives hope and healing. Dr. Len Felder explores some often-intimidating Jewish prayers, capturing their essence, and making them much more accessible. I sat down yesterday by the fire and read it from cover to cover. It's lovely."

--Craig Taubman
Award-winning Singer/Songwriter
"Friday Night Live" and "One Shabbat Morning"

"Here is a refreshing and valuable book in which you can turn to virtually any page and immediately want to underline passages that strike you as significant, elevating, intriguing, and honest. Dr. Felder offers a gateway of understanding for each of the main prayers so that even someone unused to prayer could find their way to a meaningful experience. It also elevated my own prayers in our morning service. I am recommending this beautifully written book to my congregation and my students."

--Rabbi Alicia Magal
Sedona, Arizona
Author of "From Miracle to Miracle: A Story of Survival"

"From reading these enjoyable chapters, the words on the page of the prayer book suddenly take on a new meaning and can be applied to the challenges of everyday life. Dr. Felder also shares the stories of others who have used these ideas toward personal growth and healing, helping the reader to understand the power of these teachings. His personalized, honest style of writing makes me feel as though we are sitting in a room and I am having a conversation with a compassionate friend. I highly recommend this book for anyone who wishes to calm the storm in their head and move toward peace and tranquility."

--Karen Golden
Award-winning Jewish Educator and Int̶̶̶̶̶̶̶ ̶ ̶ ̶yteller

D1367719

"Beautifully written and deeply inspiring on what it means to be human in these challenging times. I love this book! It's a gift to enjoy and share with others."

--*Cantor Annie Rose, Emerita*
Temple Beth Emeth
Ann Arbor, Michigan

"This is an outstanding resource for teachers to look at the specific phrases that Dr. Felder examines, so we can inspire our students to explore their personal connection to these prayers. This thoroughly enjoyable book also provides a safe and accessible model that instructors or parents can use, encouraging their students and family members (at every level of observance and understanding) to deepen their awareness of the layers of meaning beyond the words."

--*Tami Weiser*
Head of School, Stephen Wise Temple, Los Angeles
Member, Partnership for Excellence in Jewish Education

"Felder shares the deep insights of a lifelong quest for the heart and soul of Jewish liturgy. He offers wise, practical advice to help readers make their own connections with prayer. Our people need this wisdom!"

--*Rabbi Mike Comins*
Author of "Making Prayer Real: Leading Jewish Spiritual Voices
on Why Prayer is Difficult and What to Do About It"
www.rabbimikecomins.com

How These Words
Can Raise Up Your Energy

How These Words Can Raise Up Your Energy

Exploring the Deeper Personal Meanings of Key Jewish Prayers

Leonard Felder, PhD

Charleston, SC
www.PalmettoPublishing.com

How These Words Can Raise Up Your Energy

First Edition

Paperback ISBN: 978-1-68515-275-8
eBook: ISBN 978-1-68515-276-5

A FEW IMPORTANT DETAILS

Pronunciations:

In this book, you will see some phonetic versions of Hebrew words so that every reader (those who know Hebrew and those who don't know Hebrew) will be able to sound out the words easily. For instance, you will see a kh in a Hebrew word such as "L'khayim" (which means "to life" as in "to life, to life, L'khayim,") and you will know that every kh in this book is for the "clearing one's throat" sound that you also find in "khutzpah," "khallah," and "Khanukah."

Stories and Vignettes:

Some of the names and identifying details in a few of the stories, examples, and vignettes have been changed to protect confidentiality, but they each are about a real individual.

Personal Care:

Since this book discusses issues like stress-management, spirituality, differing beliefs, resilience, mourning, health repair, and creative ways to stay centered during difficult moments, I urge all readers to be mindful of taking good care if you start to feel upset or uncomfortable at any point in the book. If you are currently taking any medications or working with a professional for emotional health or physical healing, please make sure to consult with your trusted care advisors if anything starts to feel too intense or agitating.

DEDICATION

This book is dedicated to my mom
Helen Rothenberg Felder

who taught me
life is fragile
and to be cherished
every morning, afternoon and evening.

CONTENTS

Introduction

All of us have moments when we feel overloaded or worn down. Or when we feel blocked creatively or stuck in a rut in some area of our lives. Or when someone at home, or at work, or in an important relationship needs us to be extra patient and compassionate, yet we are starting to feel edgy or tapped out.

At those moments, wouldn't it be great if there was a quick and profound way to reconnect with a resilience, a strength, and a flow that genuinely recharges your energy and your creativity?

This book is about tapping into a profound and highly-useful set of words, phrases, breathing techniques, and energy-boosting perspectives that come from specific Jewish prayers, meditation methods, and teachings that most of us weren't taught in much depth in our families or the classes we took as kids. You might be surprised at how they can shift your mood, your resourcefulness, and your follow-through at the exact moments when you need a genuine boost.

Feeling a Bit Distant and Unsure

Before I knew the deeper meanings and ways of connecting to the healing words and centering methods of Judaism, I often felt like I was just saying the Hebrew and English prayers in an empty, hurried way so that no one around me would discover that I wasn't sure what the words meant.

I remember as a kid in Michigan sitting next to my beloved grandfather at his traditional synagogue and wondering what the words meant that the elders were racing through. It seemed like something holy and profound might be happening in that place, but as a young child what I remember most is the hunger in my stomach for the lunch I knew they were setting up in the adjacent room. So, when I closed my eyes to pray, the words I felt in my gut were, "Please make Adon Olam happen quickly." (Adon Olam was the closing song at my grandfather's synagogue and it meant delicious food was possible very soon).

As a kid and during my teen years, I also went to services often at my family's progressive and innovative congregation where much of the service had English translations. Yet the stilted, formal translations didn't really touch my heart or inspire much connection or meaning. There was something that felt distant and impersonal about those services as well. Many of my friends and I enjoyed the social events, the summer camps and the retreat weekends where we got crushes and we sang around campfires, and we loved the repair-the-world projects of our congregation and our youth group. But we felt disconnected from many of the prayers.

Flash forward several decades. I have spent dozens of years and had hundreds of honest conversations with a variety of teachers, scholars, students, rabbis, cantors, congregants, discussion group partners, traditional Jews, progressive Jews, secular Jews, and unaffiliated Jews about how to understand the deeper levels of meaning and the profound healing and energizing possibilities of specific key phrases and Jewish mantras. Year after year I've been discovering that, as a young child, I never really understood the depth and beauty of certain words and their awesome ability to awaken our souls and boost our awareness and creativity. I am extremely grateful that now when I take a breath in and out as I say these holy words, something wonderful, uplifting, and creatively-energizing happens almost every time.

Going Deeper and Enjoying the Results

The book you are about to read has been tugging at me for many years, whispering repeatedly, "Please put this important stuff into short, easy-to-read chapters that anyone can utilize. These specific phrases are gifts that need to be shared with people, whether they already have training or are new to the brilliance of these amazing, heart-opening levels of meaning."

Each of the stories, teachings, interpretations, and methods in this book come from a several-decades search for deeper under-standing that I am hoping you will find useful and energizing for your own life and for your loved ones, especially if you (or they) have felt distant or unable to get much meaning from the Hebrew and English words that everyone around you was saying so quickly.

Please note that there are several possible ways for you and the people you care about to benefit from these chapters:

- You might be someone who frequently or occasionally goes to services and you want to be able to go deeper into what the prayers and meditations mean so that they can help you draw closer to a more profound experience of pouring out your heart, feeling part of what's going on, and finding a profound connection to what you are saying.

- You might be someone who rarely or never goes to services and yet you are a little bit curious about whether certain words and phrases might be helpful for boosting your energy, opening up your creative ideas, and connecting you with something profound and healing that you've possibly sensed when you are in nature or in quiet contemplative moments in your life.

- You might be someone who cares about being Jewish and you are worried that your kids or your grandkids, or your niece or nephew, or a few of your friends have drifted away somewhat and you wish there was some accessible book or short chapter that could help that loved one reconnect with the beauty and wisdom that they might enjoy enormously, or that might touch their heart and soul in an energy-boosting way.

- You might be a hard-working rabbi, cantor, education director, congregational leader, or teacher who wants to inspire your diverse students and congregants to discover the deeper levels of meaning and usefulness that can be found in specific prayers and meditations.

- You might be a caring parent, grandparent, sibling, friend, or colleague who sometimes gets asked what something means... and you'd like to have a good response that can spark a deep conversation or a wonderful experience of exploring together some important life-affirming themes with someone who looks to you for guidance.

In addition to each of these possible reasons for exploring this book, I would like to add one more: my goal in writing this book is to bring up-to-date and make accessible to you and your loved ones some of the most exciting and inspiring developments that have been happening in recent years to help people like you and me to dig deeper and find personal meaning and connection to the words, phrases and songs that people have raced through in the past. But now we want to know what the words mean and, most importantly, how it can open up our minds and hearts to what's possible for improving our health and repairing this world.

Please enjoy whatever you find time to read and explore in this book. Please feel free to disagree and come up with your own versions that speak to you personally. Please make sure to keep learning, to keep growing, and to keep wrestling with the beautiful words, creative interpretations, and profound phrases that can nourish our souls in so many ways.

CHAPTER ONE:

What Does It Mean
to Listen Deeply?

Have you ever been so quiet and so focused that you could hear the barely-audible pulsing sound of the universe that most of us don't notice on a busy day?

Maybe you were up in the middle of the night listening to the sound of your own breathing, or to the gentle inhale and exhale of a beloved infant or young child you were attempting to comfort so that this precious soul would be soothed and go back to sleep.

Possibly you were up early in the morning and you heard the quiet nature sounds and subtle hum of planet Earth exactly at the moment when the sunlight begins to emerge and your eyes take in the awe-inspiring first glimpses of color and detail.

Perhaps at a quiet moment on a gentle walk you were close to a river, a creek, the ocean, or a circulating fountain in someone's yard and you felt embraced by the lulling sounds of water flowing in and out.

Or you might have been sitting in a comfortable chair, or on a train, a plane, or the passenger seat of a car and there probably were some sounds or distractions around you but you closed your eyes for a few moments and you somehow found a quiet, centered place deep inside where the comforting sound of your individual breath felt connected to the pulsing breath of the universe.

One more possibility. Have you ever listened with a genuine concern to a friend, a loved one, a client, or a stranger who was telling you something vulnerable or painful and you felt deeply connected to this person and what they were describing?

Each of these are examples of "deep listening." These are quiet, conscious moments when you deliberately turn down the volume of noise and distractions from your life and you shift gently to a place of warm connection and open-hearted understanding. These are moments (either in nature, or with someone you care about, or in words that take you to a compassionate, nurturing place within you) that help you to let go of the anxious thoughts and external pressures for a few seconds, or a few minutes, so that you can hear the still, small voice of wisdom and caring that gets drowned out sometimes by all the details and uncertainties of daily life.

How Do You Get Back to That Peaceful Place?

At a stressful moment or during a busy day, or when you are anxious in the middle of the night, how do you make the shift from being bombarded by life's challenges and somehow you find a way to become fully-present, deeply insightful, and quiet enough to listen calmly to the still small voice within, or to reconnect with the invisible flow of creativity and good ideas that you have experienced at certain moments in your life.

Here's one way to get back to that peaceful, inspired feeling (that you can explore on your own or in a group of people):

Start by asking yourself, "What if there were a short meditation phrase or a centering word that could take you quickly to that deep listening place of wonderment, awe, curiosity and centered openness?

What if there were an easy-to-remember series of words that could take us to a higher level of connection, awareness and relaxed energy?"

Here's some excellent news you might not have been taught in your family or in your early education: In Judaism there is a very short and easy-to-remember phrase that most people have said many times without realizing what it means on a deeper level and how it can take you out of the stresses of daily life and instead lift you up to a place of profound curiosity and connection.

Please put your seat belt on because what I am about to describe might surprise you. Whether you know it already or not, the brief Sh'ma phrase (that will be explained carefully in the next few pages) might become your personal ticket to a beautiful, relaxed, insightful, and heart-opening experience—but only if you have some clues as to the deeper levels of meaning and connection that are found in these ancient words.

The word "Sh'ma" means "listen, hear, awaken your soul, connect with the important truths that often get drowned out by all the noise and distractions, be quiet and let something deeper emerge." It is a quite-remarkable Jewish method for centering oneself that you might find extremely useful, especially when you've been dealing with a lot of difficult moments lately.

The Traditional Interpretation

Before we go into any deeper levels of the Sh'ma phrase, let's honor the traditional translation that you probably grew up with or heard people say many times.

The traditional Hebrew words are: "Sh'ma Yisra-Eil, Adonai Eloheinu, Adonai Ekhad."

The usual English translation is "Hear O Israel, the Lord our God, the Lord is One."

If those words open up your heart in a big way and inspire you, please continue to say it the way you've always said it. I'm not asking you to fix anything if it ain't broken.

But if saying the Sh'ma has sometimes felt rote, distant, or repetitive—or if you've ever wondered if the only choice is to keep using gendered, old-school words like "Lord," or if you're unsure of what exactly does it mean when we say "is One," then how about if we go deeper and see what this profound and inspiring phrase possibly means on other levels.

One important note: Feel free to disagree or say, "No way" at any point in these next few pages. My goal is to offer you legitimate options and a deep connection to what you are saying and what it might spark within your soul. But if I go too far into something that sounds "too woo-woo for you" or if I say anything you don't like, feel free to say "Yuck" or "Not for me" or "I don't think so!" We're Jews and we always have the right to disagree and to consult with other teachers and other ways of interpreting the crucial phrases.

Exploring the Personal Impact of These Words

Here are some possible ways of translating and interpreting the Hebrew words of this short, fascinating phrase called "the Sh'ma." See which ones you like and which ones you absolutely don't like:

Let's start with the first word of the Sh'ma phrase. Most people have never slowed down sufficiently and taken a moment to listen carefully to the first audible sound of the first word of the Sh'ma. The Hebrew word Sh'ma not only means "listen" or "hear" or "connect with the quiet wisdom deep within your soul," but the shhhhhh sound at the beginning of the word Sh'ma (if you say it calmly and consciously) can physically cause you to shift into a deeper awareness if you truly open your ears for a moment to the exquisite, gentle shhhhhhhhhhhhh feeling that can remind your soul of being at peace while sitting or walking next to a river, a creek, the ocean, or the lulling sound of a well-designed fountain.

Take a moment and imitate that relaxing sound of rippling water going in and out over the pebbles, the rocks, the sand, the sides of a fountain, or the cliffs of a waterfall. Shhhhhhhh. Shhhhh. Shhhhhhhhh. It kinda makes you want to get quiet for a moment and open up to a deeper wisdom.

Or the shhhhhhh sound in Sh'ma might remind you of the human breath. The sound of a gentle, soothing, loving breath coming in to nourish you or going out to energize you. The shhhhhh sound of the gentle breath of someone who is sleeping next to you. The shhhhh sound of the relaxed breathing of someone (or a beloved pet dog or cat) you are resting with on a cozy sofa and you feel safe and connected to this supportive, sweet being.

If you listen closely for a few seconds to the shhhhhh sound of your own breath or to the shhhhhh sound of a person, a dog, or a cat that you love dearly, you might experience that this individual breath is connected somehow to the enormous pulsing breath of the universe. Each time you listen closely to your own breathing, it can draw you closer to the pulsing Breath of Life that is continually flowing in the air around you and in your own respiratory system to oxygenate your lungs, your nerves and your blood flow. In Judaism, that is one of the ways we experience our connection to the Eternal Source—that each individual person's life-force breath is somehow connected to the universal Breath of Life or Source of Life (two of the many phrases we use to describe an endless flow of energy that is beyond human descriptions).

So when you start to say the first shhhhhhh sound of the first word of the Sh'ma phrase, you are already stepping out of your routine and your stress. You are moving your awareness toward a place of relaxed breathing, heart-opening peacefulness, and connection to the Breath of Life that infuses all that exists.

What a concept that is! Your breath is your individual life support system and yet we are connected with an enormous life support system of oxygen, ions, nutrients, colors and sounds that come from an Infinite Source. We are individuals but we also have a deep connection to the widespread electromagnetic field, the continuous pulsations of the universe, the moon, the tides, the winds, the nutritious foods and the wisdom that is all around us and that originate from a place we can barely understand or describe except to call it "the In-Dwelling Presence," which in Hebrew is referred to as "the Shekhinah" (the words "In-Dwelling Presence" and "Shekhinah" are two of the other names Jewish scholars use to describe God's Presence that is beyond human descriptions).

The soothing shhhhh sound of the Sh'ma is the opposite of holding your breath or shutting down your creative energy. Instead of feeling estranged from the flow of life, the shhhh sound of the Sh'ma can assist you in opening up your heart and once again feeling connected to the creativity, the nourishment, and the good ideas for how to keep moving forward in your life. As you inhale and exhale in order to say the "shhhhhhh'ma" with a calm centeredness, notice if your mind and body are starting to feel a little less stressed and a little more open.

Making Room for Some Wrestling, Questioning, and Exploring

Now that the first word of the Sh'ma might possibly be reminding you to breathe more fully and comfortably, let's take a moment with the second word of the Sh'ma phrase "Sh'ma Yisra-Eil" to understand the profound meaning of "Yisra-Eil." On a globe, the word Yisrael means a country in the Middle East. In a history book, Yisrael means a people who have experienced thousands of years of celebrations and hardships. In a literal translation, Yisra means "to wrestle or strive with." Eil means God or the mysterious indescribable Source of All That Exists.

That's why the name Yisrael usually gets translated as "the ones who wrestle and strive with God."

Let's be honest here--what have your personal wrestlings been like? Have you ever disagreed, doubted, pulled away, or revised some of the ideas about God that your parents or your early teachers gave you? Have you ever felt connected for a moment to the Endless Flow of Creation or to the Creative Source, but then a minute later you started feeling separate and skeptical again? If you tend to fluctuate between belief and some skeptical questions, you are not alone. Welcome to the tribe! We're Jews—we ask a lot of questions and our tradition says, "Keep asking. Keep wrestling."

Here's one more question to consider: Have you ever felt awed or humbled at how vast and fascinating creation is and how "beyond words" the Creative Source or Underlying Wisdom seems to be—and how much we still don't know about how it all began and how it all functions on deeper levels? No wonder we are "wrestling" with these ultimate questions—they continue to be mysterious and difficult to answer definitively.

When I hear the word "Yisra-Eil" I don't think of someone aggressively wrestling (like at the Olympics or in a bar fight) or two stuffy experts egotistically competing over "who's right." I think of "wrestling" in the word Yisra-Eil as an intimate conversation between two study partners or two sweet souls who care about one another. Or an intimate conversation between the part of us that wants to figure things out and the part of us that humbly admits, "I don't have all the answers and I probably need to keep an open mind. There are so many possible explanations of how the universe started and how the endless creation process is still unfolding. I don't need to fixate forever on one particular answer, but in Judaism I am encouraged to keep exploring, keep asking, and keep discussing these topics from a place of mutual respect for each person's unique piece of insight into the vast puzzle."

Wrestling (in a Jewish spiritual context) is not about "winning" or "squashing someone," but rather about "engaging," "exploring together," "disagreeing in a caring way," or "turning it over and over so that we can see what we didn't see previously." That's why I urge you to please be loving and kind to your own sweet questioning soul and to the sweet questioning soul of the people you are conversing with in your family and your circle of friends. One of the things I love about being Jewish is when a compassionate rabbi, teacher, parent, sibling, friend, or colleague takes a breath and is willing to honor and listen to the wrestlings and disagreements that we all bring to the conversations about what really matters in life. Yes, we tend to have a lot of intense discussions, but hopefully these explorations are a way to help each of us to dig deeper, to learn, and to grow (rather than a competition over who has "the one and only right answer" or who is going to dominate).

The Third Word of the Sh'ma that is a Mystery to This Day

Now it starts to get even more interesting and intriguing. The third word of the Sh'ma phrase is usually spoken aloud as "Adonai," which often gets translated as "Lord." But here we need to look at what's actually in the original Hebrew in every Torah scroll written by a trained scribe. It doesn't really say "Adonai" in the original Hebrew. The third word in the Sh'ma prayer is the four consonant (no vowels) word "Yud Hei Vov Hei."

Many scholars suggest that the words "Adonai" or "Lord" do not quite capture the whole truth about what "Yud Hei Vov Hei" means, which is better translated as "what is, what was, and what will be." Rather than just a male landlord or king sitting on a throne (which made a lot of sense to Jews long ago when they were very familiar with feudal landlords and kings who sat on thrones), the Yud Hei Vov Hei ("what is, what was, and what will be") is more like an endless flow of wisdom and creative bursts, more like an enormous, life-sustaining river of insights and nutrients, or possibly an energizing atmospheric wind of creative energy going from past to present to future and infusing all that exists.

Yud Hei Vov Hei can possibly be understood in a deeper way if you look at the Torah text in the Book of Exodus where Moses says to the Divine Source, "When the people ask me what to call you, what should I tell them" and Moses hears the Infinite Voice say, "Ehi-yeh ah-sheir ehi-yeh," which can be translated as "I am becoming what I am becoming" or "I am constantly changing, expressing, creating, guiding, interacting." That is a quite different possibility than just a male gendered "Lord." It's much more like a non-gendered process of continually flowing (in some mysterious and hard-to-describe way) from the past, into the present, and forward to the future.

So when you close your eyes and say the Sh'ma to get sufficiently quiet in order to activate your deep listening and your deeper wisdom, imagine for a moment that you are connecting with the Infinite Flow of Ongoing Creation that infuses everything that exists. You can still call this Infinite Flow by the name "Adonai" or "Lord." Or you can call this Infinite Flow the "Creative Source," "The Breath of

Life," "The Source of Life," "HaShem, the Name that is beyond our human words," or the "Yud Hei Vov Hei, what is, was, and will be."

I don't claim to know the one and only answer with absolutely certainty of what YHVH is going to mean for you and for your loved ones. That's for you and your loved ones to explore and decide without anyone judging or criticizing your decisions. All I know for sure is that in my own quiet moments of saying the Sh'ma with a sense of openness and curiosity, I tend not to picture the angry old man with white hair and a lightning bolt you see in some famous paintings, but rather I take a deep breath in and out as I seek to align my soul and my actions with the Endlessly Flowing Energy, Soul, and Guidance of the Universe (which are other names for God in respected Jewish teachings that humbly admit our human words cannot fully pinpoint exactly how God functions).

Is It Okay to Use the Translation That Speaks to Your Unique Soul?

Now that we've begun to explore (while translating the Sh'ma phrase) a few of the many names and interpretations for the mysterious Source of All That Exists, we need to make room for a couple of crucial questions you or a loved one might be asking: "Is it okay in Judaism to translate the Hebrew words in a way that opens up your heart and feels authentic to you even if that translation is different from what you grew up with? Is it okay to use the not-quite-literal translation that speaks to your unique soul?"

That decision (traditional translations or more personal translations) is up to you and the people you trust the most for advice on spiritual issues. It's not up to me to tell you what's okay or not okay.

But what I can say is that throughout Jewish history there have been an enormous number of teachings, rulings, and guidance that say it's perfectly okay to dig deeper into hidden meanings and to seek the translations and interpretations that ring true for you personally.

For example, there is a widely-agreed-upon belief in Judaism that each individual has a slightly different perspective or piece of the puzzle on how to connect with the mysterious Creative Source of the Universe. We know this because of numerous rabbinic commentaries and teachings about a specific verse in the opening paragraph of "The Great Prayer," (which is often called "The Amidah" or "The Standing Prayer" that gets recited daily and on every Sabbath).

Consider this: The opening paragraph of The Great Prayer says, "God of Abraham, God of Isaac, God of Jacob" (and in many modern prayer books you will also see "God of Sarah, God of Rebecca, God of Rachel, God of Leah").

That repetition of the words "God of this individual" and "God of that individual" (rather than the simpler and less wordy "God of Abraham, Isaac, Jacob, Sarah, Rebecca, Rachel and Leah") would make a grammar expert (or any person who likes efficiency or Marie Kondo clutter-free home design) cringe or say "What!! Why in this 'Standing Prayer' does each of the beloved ancestors have a different, two-extra-words 'God of' phrase mentioned for the One God?"

The answer (about "God of this individual" and "God of that individual" each needing a separate acknowledgment in the Standing Prayer) that you will find in many Jewish writings and teachings is that each of our beloved ancestors and each of us today have a slightly different connection or inner sense of the One God which is beyond human description. In each unique person and in each new generation, there are additional insights and moments of clarity about how the world works and what might be the Creative Process or Source that Flows Through All That Exists.

That's why there are many different methods recommended by well-respected rabbis, teachers, scholars, writers and congregants for how to make the Hebrew and English words about the mysterious "Yud Hei Vov Hei" more accessible, more inspiring, and thought-provoking. Each century, each decade, and each year there are new insights and new ideas about how to understand and connect in an honest way to the holy energies that are so hard to describe.

For instance, I remember in my late 20's I attended a standing-room-only conference at the University of Judaism in Los Angeles (now called American Jewish University) where there were over a thousand rabbis, teachers, scholars, students, and congregants from all over the world (Orthodox, Conservative, Reform, Reconstructionist, Renewal, Secular, and Unaffiliated) passionately discussing how to help Jews of all types to feel more connected to the poetic and prayerful words of Jewish tradition. I happened to be sitting next to a woman whose nametag said, "Marcia Falk, PhD." She was friendly and extremely wise on a number of topics, especially art, literature, history, and Hebrew word origins. I didn't know at the time that Marcia Falk had studied at Jewish Theological Seminary in New York, at Brandeis University in Massachusetts, at Stanford University in California, and at Hebrew University in Jerusalem, or that she had been invited to speak and teach at numerous colleges and at the rabbinic seminaries that train Conservative, Reform, and Reconstructionist Jews.

I just knew that she was the friendly woman sitting next to me for an entire day of speakers and that she and I had some long wonderful conversations about a book she was in the early stages of writing. That book, entitled "The Book of Blessings," came out a few years later and it had an enormous impact on helping Jews all over the world to start conversations about her gender-free, quite-poetic prayer translations that added tremendous beauty and deep meaning to many of the existing prayers.

Like many other Jewish scholars and teachers in recent years, Dr. Marcia Falk was opening up new and inspiring ways of understanding the Hebrew and English words. She told me during our one-on-one conversations (and I later saw in each of her books) that it's possible and consistent with many Jewish scholars and rabbinic teachings to connect with the Divine Presence not just as "Lord" or "King" but also as "Source of Life," "Fountain of Blessings," or "Breath of Life" and that this mysterious "Source of Blessings and Wisdom" might be continually available to us to connect with if we study and learn the ways of aligning with that "Endless Flow of Creativity and Nourishment." The thought-provoking prayers and phrases in Marcia Falk's writings are an opening gateway for anyone who has wanted to find inspiring words that touch the heart and awaken the senses.

Eight years later, I met and became friends with a compassionate and brilliant teacher from Boulder, Colorado named Rabbi David Cooper who also taught me some important deeper perspectives from Jewish sources about how to translate the Hebrew words and phrases. Rabbi Cooper was an American Jew who had studied for many years with numerous Jewish mystical rabbis and teachers in Tzefat, Israel who carefully explained and explored with Rabbi Cooper the profound meanings of many of the traditional prayers and phrases.

A few months before I met Rabbi Cooper at a Shabbat dinner at someone's home, he had published a book I enjoyed a lot about how to be more mindful, compassionate and fully alive while practicing the Jewish traditions of prayer, ritual, and generosity. I imagined before that Shabbat dinner that I would be meeting a "famous author," but in fact I quickly discovered that Rabbi David Cooper was a down-to-earth, very warm and accessible human being.

Since Rabbi Cooper was beginning work on a new book and my first job after graduating from Kenyon College in Ohio had been at Doubleday Publishing in New York, he and I began a series of conversations in person and on the phone over the next few years about how to deal with opinionated book company executives and how to navigate the process of getting editors, the sales department, the "suits" in the business department, and the anxious publishing division vice president to honor your authentic voice rather than having to make too many commercially-driven edits that diminished the truth about what you are writing.

The enormously impactful book that Rabbi David Cooper slowly birthed into the world a few years later after much labor and some excellent rewrites was called "God is a Verb." It became a highly-praised and well-received bestseller worldwide and it inspired many rabbis, teachers, students, and congregants from all the branches of Judaism to begin to consider God not as "a thing," "a noun," "an it," or a "he" or a "she," but rather to explore what the ancient and modern Jewish mystics have been trying to tell us—that God is more likely a flow, a process, an endless series of expansions, contractions and continually-available guidance and energy—that pulses and infuses all of creation, including our human souls. According to the ancient Jewish mystics and to contemporary scholars like Rabbi David Cooper and many others, the Always-Expressing Source is more like a continuous action (a verb) and less like a static, fixed object (a noun).

So when you look at the Sh'ma phrase and you hear people saying the word "Adonai" and the translation in English says, "Lord," feel free to say it the way you've always said it or possibly to experiment with something new (and know that there are thousands of Jewish scholars, teachers, rabbis, and congregants who are whispering in your ear, "Go further. Reach into your heart and connect with the endless, gender-free flow of nourishing energy and deep wisdom)."

Is that an experience you have already had or would like to have now or in the future—to listen deeply and connect with a gender-free flow of nourishing energy and deep wisdom? Please take a moment to consider what that would be like for you in your daily life—to feel more connected and more closely aligned with the Creative Flow, or to the Infinite Wisdom, or to the Pulse of the Universe? As you gently breathe in and out right now for a few seconds, please listen ("Sh'ma") to the silent but powerful Infinite Breath that is constantly connecting, guiding, and trying to repair this fragile and unfinished world.

The Fourth Word

The next word in Sh'ma is "Elo-hei-nu, our God," which in Judaism is a mystery we don't turn into a picture or a human-like being, but rather we say in honesty that God is beyond what any us can figure out completely and that's why many Jews call God "Ha-Shem," which means the Name that is beyond human labels or human words.

Because the word "Elo-hei-nu" has the suffix "nu" at the end of it, and in Hebrew a "nu" suffix means "our" or "that which is dear or beloved to us," it has a warmth and a closeness that adds to the feeling. We might not be able to pinpoint exactly how vast or how profound God is, but we can still feel a sense of closeness and warmth to what we personally believe about the Continually-Expressing Source of All That Exists.

But what if the words "Eloheinu, our God" feel a little uncomfortable or inaccessible to you? It's quite possible that a particular pushy someone in your past tried to force you to believe or practice something that you didn't believe or want to practice. So there might be some hesitation about this topic, or some pain or unpleasant memories inside you about concepts as hard-to-define as the word "God."

In addition, quite often I meet people who are highly-educated or scientific and they were told by one of their science professors or colleagues that there is a permanent split between science and believing in God. But in Judaism for many centuries there has been a coming together of scientific research, new discoveries, and how these insights give us additional clues to our understanding of the Ultimate Source of Life, which we call "our God." Instead of being afraid of scientific discoveries or disregarding them, most Jewish scholars, rabbis, and teachers today are finding that science and belief quite often are in alignment and that the old split between hard science and deep faith is no longer true or relevant.

For example, I remember going to the beautiful town of Tzefat in Israel and spending some time meditating quietly in the small, carefully-preserved synagogue where Rabbi Isaac Luria spoke to his congregation 500 years ago about how creation possibly started with a large explosion of light that was too intense and so the Creative Source had to pull back somewhat and make room for humans to be partners in repairing the world ("tikkun olam") and healing all the shards of hidden light and brokenness in this world from that initial, much-too-intense burst of light.

Over four hundred years later, a number of acclaimed scientists throughout the world began to seek proofs for the concept of the Big Bang, an initial burst of light that possibly created this world and also left a lot of chaos, brokenness, and "dark matter" that is invisible but comprises a large portion of what holds the world together. It's quite amazing how a belief from 500 years ago in Tzefat (about how God created this world with an enormous burst of light and why we need tikkun olam--our participation in repairing the brokenness), can be described almost identically by scientists in the current century. I find it very helpful to keep learning and exploring how numerous Jewish teachings and scientific discoveries (when you put them together) keep giving us crucial guidance about how the hard-to-define "our God and God's human partners" participate daily in the ongoing repair and healing of the world we live in.

So when you say the word "Eloheinu, our God" in the Sh'ma phrase, please be gentle with yourself regarding any old wounds, discomforts, or uncertainties you might have on these issues. But also, please take a moment to make sure to look deep inside for what you are exploring right now about the Endless Flow and whether there is an important partnership that we humans have in repairing this fragile world and helping to care for the vulnerable creations we see all around us.

The Final Unifying Word

At the end of the Sh'ma phrase, the last word is Ekhad, which means oneness, unity, inclusion, infusion into every individual being, or the ultimate energy source and profound wisdom which connects all that exists. The Sh'ma phrase is inviting us to break free of our lonely separateness and awaken to the fact that we are part of an amazing whole that is continually changing, developing, and unfolding.

Does that ring true for you? Have you ever glimpsed some of the ways you are part of an Ekhad, a oneness, a wholeness? For example:

- Do you sometimes feel that you are not just your isolated, anxious self, but that you might also be part of something greater and much more interconnected—that there is a positive reason why you woke up today or a useful purpose you have the chance to fulfill?

- Have you ever felt that one of your actions (for example, when you give a donation to a helpful cause) has ripple effects that go far and wide, perhaps much farther and wider than you can see with your own eyes to impact individuals and families you might never meet in person or hear about directly? It might feel to you like your contribution was just a drop in the bucket, but in fact you are part of a much larger oneness or wholeness (an Ekhad) that is slowly shifting because of each person's individual contributions.

- Have you ever been in nature or in a large gathering of compassionate people and wondered, "Am I just one person alone in the world, or am I part of some bigger picture or shared creation that is about working together for healing and repair?" Have there been moments when you felt surrounded by beauty or goodness in a worthwhile project and, as a result, you didn't feel so separate, alone, or powerless?

Rather than feeling trapped in your isolated, noisy brain or being limited by the aches and pains of your body, the Sh'ma phrase says, "Hey, open up. You are part of something bigger, something that is interconnected with all sorts of good flows of energy and ways of being useful and helpful in the world. Take a breath and align yourself in a small or large way with the forces for compassionate change in this world."

Or here's another possible way to understand what is meant by Ekhad or oneness in the Sh'ma phrase we tend to say so quickly sometimes:

Many years ago I read the fascinating book "The Jew in the Lotus" by Rodger Kamenetz about how a group of contemporary rabbis traveled to India to help the exiled Tibetan Buddhist leader, The Dalai Lama, to explore numerous good ideas on how to keep a spiritual tradition alive and thriving even if you have to spend more than a thousand years dispersed away from your homeland (like what the Jewish people have experienced for many, many centuries and what the Chinese government has been forcing the Tibetan Buddhists to do the past seventy years in exile from their historic homeland).

A few years later after reading about The Dalai Lama's very honest and fascinating dialogues with numerous rabbis and Jewish historical experts, I went to see The Dalai Lama in person. I liked much of what he said and disagreed on some specific points. But like most people, I truly enjoyed seeing his enormous sense of humor, his profound playfulness, and his respect for diverse beliefs. So I hope he wouldn't mind if I pass along to you a humorous story about The Dalai Lama, which beautifully relates to the final word "Ekhad, one-ness," in the Sh'ma phrase of Judaism.

In this humorous story, The Dalai Lama is visiting Manhattan and he sees the hard-working vendors in Central Park who are roasting chestnuts, onions, peppers, and other foods on their portable carts. One particular vendor, an in-your-face street entrepreneur from Brooklyn, says in a hurried voice to The Dalai Lama, "Hey fella, you're next! What do you want!"

The Dalai Lama closes his eyes, takes a breath in and out, and says to the vendor with kindness, "What I really want is if you could make me one with everything."

If you didn't get the joke on the first try, please feel free to read the previous sentence one more time: the Dalai Lama closes his eyes, takes a deep breath in and out, and says to the vendor with kindness, "What I really want is if you could make me one with everything."

The Sh'ma phrase (especially the word Ekhad, oneness) is our Jewish way of saying, "Please make me one with everything. Please help me to be aware that there is Ekhad, a unity and a wholeness that connects all that exists."

Even if it's just for one brief, amazing moment—can you imagine yourself saying the Sh'ma and connecting with an all-embracing flow of energy that is vast and profound?

Maybe you've already experienced a glimpse of what it feels like to be connected to "the oneness of all of creation" if you've ever listened to the wind on a mountaintop as you looked out toward the vastness; or listened to the waves in front of the ocean, or along a river, or at a waterfall when you experienced the breezes and sounds embracing you. Or possibly you experienced a quick moment of deep connection and oneness with someone you care about deeply. Or you felt a sense of oneness and harmony when you were singing with a group of people and the combined sounds lifted you up. Or when you were involved in a creative project and you felt fully alive and truly "in the flow." These are unforgettable moments when you are no longer isolated or shut down, but instead you feel part of the "inclusive One" or the "continuously-flowing Breath of Life." They are moments when you experience a sense of "Ekhad, oneness."

Saying It with Genuine Feeling

Now that we've deconstructed and explored what the words of the Sh'ma mean on various levels, let's stop the analyzing for a moment and just try out a few ways to say it with genuine feeling and openness.

I'll offer you a few ways to say the Sh'ma with an open heart and a deeper connection. But I also invite you to come up with your own personal words and translations.

Here's one possibility:

Sometimes when I say the Sh'ma, I don't even translate the words. I just cover my eyes, take a gentle breath in and out, and then listen with curiosity to the quiet that is deep inside and all around me in order to wait patiently and see what emerges.

Or another possibility:

Sometimes I take a breath and say silently a translation that stirs up curiosity and connection. As I breathe in and out slowly, I sometimes say in a very quiet voice, "Sh'ma Yisra-Eil, Adonai Eloheinu, Adonai Ekhad," and I translate it as, "Listen deeply, sweet questioning soul, because the Creative Source is flowing and open right now for connecting. Listen deeply and open up to the One." Then I do my best to be very quiet for a moment and see what emerges.

Or another possibility:

Sometimes I say a much shorter version, such as, "Listen deeply right here to the One that is continuously flowing and guiding us," and I stay quiet for a few moments to see what happens.

Now it's your turn to explore various translation possibilities. You are free to try out the specific words listed above that I've found useful to see if they feel helpful to you or not. Or please take a moment to find your own particular way of breathing into the words "Sh'ma—listen deeply," or "Yisra-Eil—your sweet questioning soul," or "Adonai Eloheinu—what is your personal sense of the Creative Force that flows through you and all around you," or "Ekhad—what is your unique way of feeling connected and energized by the One that weaves together all that exists."

Please don't feel you have to settle for only the translations and interpretations I have listed in this chapter. If there is a rabbi, a cantor, a teacher, a study partner, a friend, or a family member that you respect and feel good about, please reach out to that person and ask them to explore with you how you can say the Sh'ma phrase with depth and authenticity to re-energize your soul whenever your soul feels depleted or drained by the many pressures and demands in your life.

The Sh'ma is such a fascinating short phrase of just a few words that are easy to memorize. Please turn it over and turn it over until you find your unique way of nourishing your connection to the energetic Source that lights up and inspires all who call out to that Source. I have found that with each passing year, my appreciation of this centering, energizing phrase keeps growing the more I learn about it.

A Few Quick Examples that Might Be Useful to You or a Loved One

To close this chapter, I want to describe briefly just a few real-life variations of the possible ways that I have heard people benefit from saying and deeply feeling the Sh'ma phrase in their daily lives, at services, or in their desire to live more mindfully and lovingly. Please consider whether any of these quick, real-life illustrations might spark your own personal explorations:

The Middle-of-the-Night Moments

Are you ever awakened for some reason in the middle of the night and you find it's difficult to fall back to sleep? Some of my counseling clients (Jewish or not Jewish) have benefited from saying the Sh'ma as a soothing, calming way to unhook and let go during those middle-of-the-night moments. Instead of feeling at 3 a.m. or 4 a.m. that you immediately need to solve every issue that's running through your head, there is something freeing and helpful that happens when you take a few gentle breaths in and out as you hear the soft, silent words of "Sh'ma, listen to the silence." In that moment of just breathing calmly and letting go as you connect with the silent

Breath of Life, you might sense that there is a Oneness that is keeping the world flowing even when you and I are off-duty, and right now we can just relax into that soothing flow for the next few hours. As you breathe gently in and out, you can rely on the fact that the sunlight will re-emerge in the morning, and at that time you'll be better able to deal with things in full daylight.

What would that be like for you? To simply breathe and slowly let go as you listen to the calming silence around you, rather than the noise inside your brain? What would it feel like to allow your individual breath to be soothed by the vast Breath of the Universe that is flowing always?

The Return to Services

A second example of the usefulness of the Sh'ma is when it allows you to hear the deepest desires of your soul. One afternoon in my office, I was talking with a counseling client who is a very insightful and creative woman in her mid-30's who grew up in a Jewish family but rarely goes to services except occasionally on the High Holidays.

On that afternoon during her counseling session about her complicated extended family, she was discussing the fact that she had been invited to her niece's bat mitzvah on an upcoming weekend and she asked me for a suggestion on how she could make it more meaningful than usual for the time she would be at those services. We had been talking about some of the difficult family members who would be at that bat mitzvah and how she was going to deal with these particular individuals in a graceful way. But now this counseling client was asking specifically for how to make the time spent at services more enjoyable and more meaningful.

I asked her what it's been like for her in the past when she attended a service and she admitted, "I usually don't get much meaning or connection to what's being said. I often get bored and look at my watch several times."

I appreciated her honesty and we talked about some of her mixed feelings about religion and spirituality in general. Then I asked her if there was any particular song or prayer phrase that she'd ever found intriguing or that she was curious about.

She thought for a moment and then told me, "I've always wondered why people seem so focused and moved by the Sh'ma. I've noticed a bunch of people, even some who are well-dressed and quite sophisticated, tend to cover their eyes and go deep into a meditation state or something like that when they say the Sh'ma. Why does it seem so moving to some people and so rote or empty for others?"

In response to her question, we talked for a few minutes about the Sh'ma and how various different people connect with it. I asked this highly-intelligent and very honest woman, "How about if you try an experiment at your niece's bat mitzvah. Just focus for a few minutes on the word, 'Sh'ma, listen deeply' and see what happens inside you. See if you can use just that one peaceful word 'Sh'ma, listen….' as a gateway that allows you to hear the important longings and genuine concerns that are found deep in your soul, or to listen with curiosity to the quiet, mysterious silence as you gently breathe in and out. Or possibly when you say 'Sh'ma, listen lovingly,' you might experience some very personal curiosities and feelings that come up as you are surrounded by people praying and singing. Even if no insights or breakthroughs pop into your mind, it might just be a moment to break free of the pressures and agitating thoughts that berate us each week, so that you can have at least a few exquisite, nourishing seconds of going to a place of calmness and connection."

A week later, this counseling client came into my office and told me, "Uh-oh, I never thought I'd be saying this, but I might be going

back to services a few more times in the near future. I was quite surprised that I felt a little more relaxed and somewhat moved when I
took a few breaths, covered my eyes, and joined in the soft chant and
spontaneous moment of listening carefully while saying the Sh'ma
in a genuine way that I had never done before. It was somewhat
calming to my nerves and it got me wondering why I very rarely take
the time, or get quiet enough, to be able to listen to the feelings and
questions that are deep within me. I guess I'm usually too busy or
too much in a hurry to check in with the quiet voice inside me that
wants to be heard. At the services where my niece was leading some
of the prayers and doing her interpretation of the weekly Torah portion, I realized I can unhook somewhat from the pressures of the
week and give myself permission to slow down, to be quiet, to enjoy
the melodies, and to listen to what's going on inside me. It made
me want to try that out a few more times—to put myself in a place
where it's okay to cover your eyes, to breathe calmly, and to remind
myself to listen to what I'm usually too busy to hear."

The Man Who Works with Irate People

Finally, here is one additional and very-practical example of how the
Sh'ma can be helpful and transformative. I have a longtime friend
who is a hard-working manager in a highly-stressful company where
almost every day he has to deal with at least one or more irate cus-
tomers, clients, colleagues, bosses, or computer techs who tend to
snap at him or go ballistic when there's a problem or when there's a
turf battle or power struggle between strong-willed individuals.

A few months ago, my friend and I were talking about this chapter that I was starting to write about the Sh'ma phrase and how
effective it is for helping people to shift from a feeling of overwhelm
or agitation, and instead opening up to a feeling of calmness and the

ability to listen with an open heart whenever someone at work or in your personal life is irate, demanding, or intense.

My friend was skeptical about whether a short phrase like the Sh'ma could have much usefulness or effectiveness in the middle of a tense conversation or a recurring power struggle with someone in your daily life. So we made a bet with each other to test the effectiveness of the Sh'ma phrase.

For just one week, my friend (as part of the bet) was going to say to himself, "Sh'ma listen deeply" each time he was in a heated or rushed conversation with an irate individual at work. Then he was going to see if using this mantra of "Sh'ma, listen deeply" could make him more effective in calming down his own nerves and also for calming down the irate boss, customer, client, or colleague at work.

The bet was only for $10, but that wasn't the point of the experiment. After seven days, my friend reported back to me, "It was a little surprising. I'm not someone who says a personal prayer or mantra out in the world in the middle of a tense situation. I also had no idea that using the Sh'ma phrase silently would do much at all for my nerves or my effectiveness in stressful encounters with agitated, argumentative people. But here's what happened:

"There were three different times in the past week when I tried out the Sh'ma phrase in the middle of a stressful, intense encounter with someone who had a short fuse and a condescending or angry tone of voice. While the other person was ranting, I just took a few gentle breaths in and out as I said silently to myself, 'Sh'ma, listen deeply.' I guess it caused the other person to realize that I wasn't being defensive or dismissive. Instead, the words 'Sh'ma, listen,' that I said silently to myself, allowed me to be calm enough to let the other person sense that I truly do care and that I'm wanting to work together to come up with a viable solution to whatever has pushed this individual to the edge. I noticed that the calmer I got (and the more I could listen without getting reactive or combative), the more the other person began to lower their raised voice a little bit and not keep repeating their agitated words over and over again. So, here's your ridiculous ten dollars."

Then my friend paused and told me, "It's quite something to be able to turn a tense, ugly situation around just by silently having a couple of quick, gentle words I can say to myself that changes the way I listen, and sometimes causes the other person to feel heard and included. I told my wife about the ten-dollar bet and about what happened at work when the Sh'ma phrase helped me dis-arm three different people who had short fuses."

My friend then added, "After I told her I'd lost the ten-dollar bet, my wife got a mischievous smile on her face and she whispered that she was a little bit glad that I lost the bet. Then she looked straight into my eyes as she said playfully, 'Okay, now would you be willing at home with me and our teenage daughter to be a little less defensive or 'too busy to really listen'. Maybe you could say your quick words—'Sh'ma listen deeply'--to yourself when we're trying to get you to hear us with an open heart. Instead of saying what you usually say, 'Cut to the chase' or 'Get to the point,' or becoming defensive and impatient like you've told me your father used to do toward you when you were a kid, what if you reminded yourself to just listen lovingly and you took a relaxing breath and really opened up to what we're trying to discuss with you. That would help prevent so many of the tense moments and hurt feelings that have been happening lately in our home. We love you and we know you love us, but that impatient way you cut us off at least once a day is not easy to put up with. If you could calmly say to yourself 'Sh'ma, listen deeply' and then quickly be more fully present, that would be a breakthrough for all of us."

What About You and Your Loved Ones?

Whether you decide to experiment with the Sh'ma phrase when you are at services, at work, or at home with your loved ones, or having difficulty falling back to sleep in the middle of the night, or when you are taking a walk or out in nature, I hope it helps you experience the shift from "agitated thoughts" or "anxious impatience" to a more enjoyable feeling of "calmness, connection, deep listening, and openness."

It might take a few times of practicing the words until they become completely comfortable for you. But I have found repeatedly that when good people use this quick and profound phrase to break free of their noisy brains and instead connect with a profound sense of genuine listening and comforting wholeness, it can have wonderful results.

I am hoping you and your loved ones will have many exquisite Sh'ma moments of hearing and enjoying the flow of creativity and the flow of compassion that is available whenever we tap into it. Please try it out a few times on your own, or in a group of caring people at services, to explore what it feels like from now on to be fully open, to be listening calmly, and to be growing and learning always.

CHAPTER TWO

How Do You Get from Tiredness to Gratitude?

If you ask a hundred people if they feel rested, energetic, and happy first thing in the morning, you will probably find that the vast majority of individuals tend to experience some grogginess, anxious thoughts, occasional sadness, or a little bit of spaciness when they first wake up.

How about you? What are you like first thing in the morning when your hair isn't combed, your eyelids are a little bit heavy, and your thoughts are somewhat scattered or negative? What's it like for you on stressful weeks when you get woken up suddenly and your body is saying, "Could I have a little more sleep, please?" or "Do I really have to get up and deal with a certain frustrating person or upsetting situation again today?"

It's perfectly normal to feel some tiredness. Especially if you have an intense job (or if you are in between jobs and there are bills to pay). Or you might feel sluggish and resistant in the morning if you have loved ones, roommates, or friends who sometimes get on your nerves. Or you might feel like you would prefer some extra sleep if you have encountered some setbacks lately in your life. Or you might find yourself ruminating for a while before getting up if you have some cherished goals and quests that have gotten sidetracked or postponed lately.

Now here's something interesting to consider if you want to understand why your brain is so filled with worries, frustrations, and concerns every so often (especially first thing in the morning): If you have an anxious brain at the start of many of your days, you are truly not alone. In fact, there is scientific proof that the human brain is hard-wired to constantly look for problems to solve and things that are incomplete or frustrating.

This crucial scientific fact that nearly every human brain tends to ignore or take for granted what's going well or what's basically okay (and instead that the human brain is like a problem-seeking device that starts each day ruminating about problems and worries) came from an amazing woman scientist several decades ago named Bluma Zeigarnik. Dr. Zeigarnik was a Jewish woman who broke into the male-dominated field of research-oriented experimental psychology with a curiosity for how the brain decides what to focus on, as opposed to what the brain tends to ignore or take for granted. Dr. Zeigarnik created some carefully-designed experiments to assess what our brains notice and remember, versus what our brains tend to dismiss or forget. Her discovery, which is known by most psychologists and brain researchers as "the Zeigarnik Effect," holds the key to whether your life starts to feel like an endless string of frustrating problems or whether you can find a way to enjoy numerous moments of happiness and thankfulness.

Briefly summarized, the Zeigarnik Effect is the scientific demonstration that your brain and my brain are hard-wired to look for what is troublesome or incomplete, or what needs to be solved or fixed. When Bluma Zeigarnik showed a large number of people a circle that was 7/8 complete, the eyes and the thoughts of most people in the lab study focused on the 1/8 of the circle that was incomplete. When Bluma Zeigarnik gave a series of phrases and sentences to a large number of study volunteers, they tended to forget or not focus on the phrases that were perfectly fine and at the same time their brains focused much more vigilantly and remembered much more easily the one or two words that were mixed up or confusing. Her carefully-designed studies of human focusing patterns revealed for the first time that our human brains constantly tend to search for something that's not okay and then to try to solve that problem (and sometimes obsess about that problem).

In some ways this might be a good thing for basic survival, because it's often useful to have a perpetual-problem-seeking-device inside your skull that can sense danger, look for trouble, and then figure things out and fix things that are incomplete or broken (especially since so many things in this world and in our human interactions are troublesome, incomplete, or broken).

But sadly (according to Bluma Zeigarnik's research and the research of many other scientists), our brains are pretty lousy at noticing what's already okay or what's solid, complete, joyful, or dependable. Our problem-seeking brain is not very likely to notice or take to heart some important and genuine things like gratitude, or what's mostly okay, or what's better now than it was before, and especially what is in our life right now that we can feel good about or positive about. It's rather unfortunate that our brains (and the brains of the people we live with and work with) so often tend to forget, ignore, or take for granted the absolutely true things that could be bringing us a sense of happiness or forward momentum—because our brains are constantly rushing into trying to chase after the next unsolved problem.

If you want to understand why your thoughts tend to go negative or anxious so often, imagine that your brain is like the scheduling director at a news station or an internet news-feed, demanding each day, "Get rid of the feel-good, positive stories. We want more fires, floods, scandals, car chases, and things to worry about. Those are what make people watch or listen much more vigilantly."

Is It Possible to Over-ride the Brain's Built-In Sense of Worry and Agitation?

If you have ever wanted to become more adept at feeling more alive each day (and less drained or burned out by the hard-to-resolve dilemmas of daily life), you will need to have a method or a tool for dealing with the fact that we each have a brain that is somewhat addicted to bad news and anxious thoughts. What if there were an easy-to-use remedy for helping our problem-seeking brain to be more successful at noticing and enjoying what's also going well or that might bring us a sense of happiness or forward momentum?

Now here's some good news that is also very practical and doable: Starting numerous centuries ago and continuing to the present decade, a series of insightful rabbis and innovative Jewish scholars have come up with a way to outsmart the problem-obsessed human brain that can't seem to recall what's going well, that worries too much, and that can't fully experience much of the pleasure or gratitude from our daily lives.

Are you interested in knowing the secret sauce that possibly can make each day substantially more delicious, more energized, and less drained by the worrying ways of the problem-seeking missile we each have behind our foreheads?

It's called "The Path of Blessing" and it's something you can do quickly or slowly (depending on how much time you have in your morning and throughout the day). Here's how it works:

The Motivation

In order to decide whether you want to explore and utilize some version of "The Path of Blessing," please take a moment to ask yourself these questions:

- What if I were able to start each morning a little more positive and a little less tired or groggy than I've been experiencing lately?

- What if there were a do-able way I could quickly shift my mood or my thoughts from a sense of overwhelm or frustration, and instead feel connected to a flow of good energy, great ideas, deep wisdom, and nourishment that I can bring into all the challenging situations I am facing on a busy day?

- What if I knew precisely how to reclaim and take to heart the enjoyable things and the exquisite moments that my problem-seeking brain tends to ignore, dismiss, or forget so quickly?

- What if I could test out and see for myself if saying "thank you for this wonderful thing that I usually overlook or take for granted" can make a noticeable difference in my energy levels and how resilient I can be on a tough day or a tough week?

The rabbis and Jewish scholars in previous centuries and in current times who designed a way to outsmart the never-satisfied, problem-obsessed, anxious human brain have given us a quick and effective method for essentially turning on the light switch inside the barely lit parts of our brains that are connected to creativity, innovation, enjoyment, balance, and thankfulness. You and I now have the opportunity (one day at a time, one hour at a time, one minute at a time) to test out this "Path of Blessing" to see whether it works in our own stressful lives.

The Early Morning Possibilities

For many centuries, the rabbinic words and phrases in the Path of Blessing have been used by numerous individuals as soon as they are beginning to emerge from sleep in the morning. Instead of waking up being deluged by problems, worries, ruminations, and insecurities, the Path of Blessing starts with a simple phrase you can say even if your eyes are barely open and your body is still partially resting.

The opening phrase that you can say to yourself to significantly boost your energy for the day ahead of you is to say silently (either in these words or in your own words):

"I am so grateful that my soul is being renewed for another day. At some point today, there will be a moment when I will have a chance to do something helpful, or purposeful, or compassionate. I am truly grateful that a dependable Source is breathing life into me and allowing me to be part of the ongoing creation."

Or you can say the traditional Hebrew words (either from memory, or from a note-card, or from a screen shot on your phone next to your bed):

Here are the first two words of this mood-transforming blessing: If you identify as a woman, the first two words are: Modah ahnee—I am so grateful. If you identify as a man, the first two words are: Modeh ahnee—I am so grateful. If you identify as gender non-binary, the first two words are: Modet ahnee—I am so grateful.

What's important is that you start the day by outsmarting the problem-seeking brain and go directly to a feeling of gratitude that you have a beautiful pure soul and that your soul is being renewed for a new day of purpose and possibilities.

Here's the complete Hebrew phrase you can start each day with (from memory, or from a note-card, or from a screen shot):

Modah ahnee (or) Modeh ahnee (or) Modet ahnee (depending on whether you identify as female or male or gender non-binary)

in English it means, "I am very grateful"

L'fanekha, melekh khai v'kayam

in English it means "in front of You, Ruling Force of life and existence,"

Sheh-hekhe-zarta be nishmatee b'khemla

in English it means, "Who restores and renews my soul with compassion and purpose."

Rabbah emu-na-tekha.

in English it means, "You are dependable beyond measure."

I have found with my counseling clients, friends, and workshop participants that all sorts of diverse people (religious Jews, non-religious Jews, people from other belief systems including Christians, Muslims, Buddhists, Taoists, Hindus, Atheists, Agnostics, and others I have spoken with personally) have been willing to try out this first-thing-in-the-morning phrase and found it to be extremely helpful and energizing. It's basically saying that you are not just your messy hair or your imperfect messy house or your imperfect messy relationships—but rather you have a beautiful soul and that your soul is thankfully being renewed for another day of compassion and usefulness.

When you tap into that sense of yourself as a unique, caring soul who is here to be of service or to do some good each day, it gives you an energizing reason to wake up and feel more alive and purposeful. Even if it's been a tough week or a tough year, this new day in front of you holds the possibility that your soul is going to make an impact on at least one other soul today (or do something nurturing or protective for one small part of nature or some aspect of creation). Even if your eyelids feel heavy, you can wake up knowing that the daylight hours in front of you will have at least some definite moments of caring, creativity, or usefulness. What a radically different way to start a day than to just let your brain start obsessing on, "Are my thighs getting a little chunky lately" or "How am I going to get so and so to stop being so impatient or insensitive."

If you are new to the Modah/Modeh/Modet Ahnee phrase, please be gentle with yourself and start slowly. You might want to begin each morning by just saying silently, "I am so grateful that my soul is being renewed today for the possibility of doing something useful or compassionate." Or you might want to practice several times reading the full note-card or the screen shot with the Hebrew and/or English words and see what feelings they stir up in you about what it feels like to have a pure, unique soul…or what it's like to be open and ready to be of service each day and to start the morning consciously-primed to do something good or helpful at some point during the next twelve to sixteen hours that God or life has given you.

A Second Blessing that is Very Private and Quite Profound

There's a second quick, highly-effective phrase you can say as part of your daily "Path of Blessing" if you want to shift your brain from tiredness and grumpiness to joy and forward momentum. This second phrase, called the Bir'khat Ahsheir Yatzar ("the blessing for how our complex body is formed") is found in prayer books at every morning prayer service (weekdays, Sabbaths, and holidays) in synagogues worldwide and it also can be utilized at home. In addition, you can find this short prayer of mindfulness and thankfulness in the washrooms of certain hospitals, including Cedars-Sinai Medical Center in Los Angeles (where a friend of mine sent me a text last year that said, "Can you believe this! There's a Hebrew prayer on the placard in all sorts of washrooms here at Cedars-Sinai. What does it mean in English?")

This fascinating and mood-lifting phrase is even more ancient than the Modah Ahnee phrase described earlier. In fact, we know from the Talmud (the books of laws, interpretations, guidance, and various opinions on how to live with greater holiness and mutual respect) that a Rabbi Abaye (pronounced Ahbah-yeh) urged his students around the year 300 CE to say this short phrase silently to themselves every morning in deep gratitude.

Rabbi Abaye was born more than 1800 years ago and was orphaned at an early age. Raised by his uncle, young Abaye loved to entertain his new family by juggling and singing. He then followed in his grandfather's footsteps by becoming a scholar and rabbi at a Yeshiva academy in Pumbedita, a vibrant town in what is now Iraq.

Rabbi Abaye felt that this brief morning blessing should remind us every time we start the day that our complex bodies and our delicate inner organs were designed by a wisdom and a holy process that is truly awesome. So he encouraged people then and now to say with sincere gratitude (either when you have gone to the bathroom or when you say morning prayers at home or in the synagogue) these passionate and realistic words:

"Blessed are You, HaShem, our God, Who fashioned the human being with wisdom and created within me many openings and many cavities. It is obvious that if but one of these openings were blocked or ruptured or not open, or these closings were not closed, it would be impossible to survive and stand before You right now."

Please be aware that it's not just a thank you paragraph about going to the bathroom and saying thankfully, "Wow, it takes a lot of healthy eating habits, abundant water and fluids, and a lot of breathing and calmness to get to this successful moment." It's also a way of being mindful to the fact that our mouth, nose, throat, esophagus, intestines, stomach, kidneys, blood circulation system, and other delicate organs need to have openings and closings that don't get blocked by eating the wrong foods or not taking good care of the unique and fragile body that God or life has given you to house your soul for this lifetime.

Rather than rushing through the prayer as if it's no big deal, there is something profound and beautiful about taking a moment each morning to say, "I am aware that if my body wasn't working right now, I'd be in big trouble. So I humbly say thank you to the mysterious Creative Source that made my complex body as functional as it is and I humbly say hooray that my body is in good enough shape that I can do caring and creative things today."

For me personally, saying the words of the Ahsheir Yatzar blessing with sincerity at least once a day helps me to stay grateful for my health instead of taking it for granted or putting it in jeopardy. I learned at a very early age that I can't just assume that good health is automatic. My mom got diagnosed with cancer when she was 42 and I was 10. She died four years later. In addition, I also happen to come from a long line of folks on both my dad's side and my mom's side who had digestive problems and I discovered in my 20's that I am very allergic to dairy, wheat, corn, sugar, and greasy foods. Like many people who have inherited some digestive vulnerabilities, I realized I tend to get moderately sick for three to five days whenever I knowingly or mistakenly eat one of the foods that trigger my digestive issues (but thankfully I'm extremely healthy and productive if I remember to carefully avoid the trigger foods).

So when I say the gratitude prayer each morning for Ahsheir Yatzar ("the complex body organs, the openings and closings, that were formed for us"), I say it with enormous relief that there are doctors, nutritionists, holistic remedies, and non-allergic foods I can enjoy every day to stay healthy and to be able to take good care of my loved ones and do the heartfelt projects I do every day out in the world.

What about you and your loved ones:

- Do you also come from a legacy of physical challenges and vulnerabilities?

- Do you feel adept at taking excellent care of the delicate, but amazing and complex, body you have been given for this lifetime?

- Are you willing to say a short phrase of thanks or a spontaneous energy-boosting appreciation for your remarkable openings and closings that allow you to be alive, creative, and productive?

- Are you willing to set aside a few seconds each morning to say to the mysterious One that is beyond human words, "Wow! I am thankful that my body works well enough today and I'm glad to be alive!"

Some Additional Energy-Boosting Moments on the Path of Blessing

In every prayer book throughout the world (for morning services, Sabbaths, and holidays) there is also a series of short, quick Bir'khat Ha-Shakhar phrases (which in English means "The Morning Blessings") that you can say to raise up your awareness and increase your energy and strength for bringing out your best each day (rather than feeling weighed down and drained by all the challenges and frustrations in your life).

Each of these morning blessings has a similar opening phrase you can put on a note card, or save with a screen shot on your cell phone:

Ba-rukh Atah Adonai (or HaShem or Yud Hei Vov Hei)
Eloheinu Melekh Ha-Olam...

which in English usually gets translated, "Blessed are You,
Eternal our God..."

And then there's always a second phrase where we mention
something that we are grateful for or something that is an everyday
miracle or blessing that we sometimes take for granted or fail to
appreciate.

If you want to go deeper into each specific Hebrew word of
these morning prayers, there is a wonderful book that goes into detail about how to understand the process by which saying each of
these words mindfully is like turning on a spigot of good energy and
healthy resilience. The book is called "The Path of Blessing" and it
was written by a Philadelphia rabbi and longtime rabbinic-school
teacher named Rabbi Marcia Prager.

I took a half hour each morning for several weeks in 1998 to read
"The Path of Blessing" when it first got published and I loved that
it helped me understand how the morning prayers work on mystical
and spiritual levels. I didn't grow up saying the traditional morning
prayers each day in my family, but now whenever I take a few minutes to say them with a deeper understanding and appreciation for
what they mean, they consistently help me to feel much more alive
and grateful for the rest of the day.

From 1998 until 2011, I attended a few large conferences on
Jewish spirituality in various cities and found Rabbi Marcia Prager
to be an inspiring speaker on how to say prayers and blessings with
deeper intention and awareness. But these events had hundreds of
participants and I had never met Rabbi Prager close-up in person.

Then in July 2011, she and I were both scheduled to teach at
a Jewish spiritual conference for 1,200 people that was being held

on an unusually hot summer week at a college campus in the small desert town of Redlands, California. It was a short two-hour drive east for me from Los Angeles. But for many of the teachers and participants who flew in from the east coast, the south, the midwest, Canada, Israel, and Europe, it was a very stressful trip with airport delays, flight changes, luggage problems, and temperatures over 100 degrees when they got to Redlands.

As I drove up to the college dorm building where I was going to be staying for a few nights, I saw Rabbi Marcia Prager sitting on the curb in the parking lot of the dorm. I quickly learned that a friend of hers had called the paramedics. Someone told me that Rabbi Marcia Prager had flown from Philadelphia that afternoon, and in the scorching temperatures of Redlands she had shown some moderately serious symptoms of heat stroke.

I offered to help carry her bag and I watched closely in awe as Rabbi Marcia Prager calmly and compassionately spoke in a soft, soothing, grateful way to her anxious friends, her worried students, the gawking onlookers, and the hurried paramedics that she was meeting for the first time.

I've often heard it said in Jewish stories and teachings that if you sincerely want to learn about life from wise rabbis, you ought to watch them tie their shoes. Now I was standing a few feet from the author of a book that had moved me about the lifelong benefits of saying daily blessings of thankfulness and I was watching that same author gently showing gratitude, patience, and concern toward each of the people who were helping her be taken in an emergency vehicle to a desert hospital.

I cannot guarantee what will happen for you personally, or for your loved ones, if you do decide to say a few blessings and expressions of thankfulness each day to be more mindful and connected to the good flows of energy that exist in this world. But I can guarantee you that on the scorching and uncomfortable July afternoon in 2011 in the desert town of Redlands, I saw with my own eyes that Rabbi Marcia Prager was able to be centered, generous, and extremely competent as she interacted with kindness and calmness toward each of the people around her during an intense emergency situation that would have caused most other individuals to be a lot less centered and mindful.

Thankfully, Rabbi Marcia Prager recovered successfully from her heat stroke symptoms of July 2011 and she continued to teach students and numerous rabbis for many, many more years. Seeing in person how the "path of blessing" can help us walk the walk and not just talk the talk, I have re-read her book a few times because there is always more to learn about how these Jewish prayers and centering methods can boost our energy and connect us with abundant flows of creativity, gratitude, and compassion.

You don't need to be a Hebrew scholar or a long-time master of Jewish prayer rituals to experience the fascinating possibilities that can happen when you say one or more of the Bir'khat Ha-Shakhar (Morning Blessings). Here, briefly described, are just two of the other profound phrases that you can try out and see if they help you re-energize on a busy week and give you forward momentum for dealing with whatever is going on in your life on a given day.

Getting In Touch with Your Generosity and the Generosity of Others

Let's start with one of the traditional morning blessings found in every prayer book worldwide that most people race through and yet it has some fascinating and inspiring deeper meanings. It's the one that says,

"Blessed are you Eternal One, our God, who provides clothes for the naked."

In Hebrew it reads: "Ba-rukh Atah Adonai Eloheinu Melekh Ha-Olam, Mahl-beesh Ah-roo-meem."

On a surface level, it seems to be about clothes. As Gilda Radner's funny character would likely say on "Saturday Night Live":

"Clothes!!! A prayer about clothes???? Why do I need to say a prayer about clothes? What's the fuss, what's the big deal about clothes?!!!!"

To which Jane Curtin would turn to her calmly and say:

"Don't be upset, it's not just about clothes. It's about life."

And then Gilda Radner's agitated character would get quiet and say softly, "Oh." (Pause and then calmly) "Never mind…"

So let's explore the deeper levels of personal meaning of this quick blessing for "the One who provides clothing for the naked."

On a traditional level, it is usually said at the moment in the morning when a person gets out of bed and puts on some clothes to be presentable to other people or just to warm up on a chilly morning. It's a quick moment for realizing we can't take for granted that we have the privilege of putting on warm, comfortable clothes.

Have you ever stopped for a few seconds and considered what a blessing it is to be able to wear what you want to wear, and to be wrapped in warmth, comfort, and some beautiful colors? Recently, I stopped for a moment and I thought about my dad's parents in Germany, two beautiful souls named Johanna and Leopold, who had their clothes taken from them after they were rounded up and sent to Auschwitz.

I also know that my family today in 2022 is much more comfortable in many ways than my maternal grandparents and great grandparents were when they grew up without much money or possessions in small, unstable towns in the Pale of Settlement (Russian-Polish), where they certainly didn't have the chance to try on attractive new outfits at nearby clothing stores or by shopping from home and hitting the "Complete My Purchase" button at various web-sites that have excellent choices and fast deliveries.

What about you? When you think of what's in your closet, as opposed to what your great grandparents or other ancestors had in their tiny storage spaces, is it possible to feel a moment of gratitude that even with all the problems of today we are certainly not naked or lacking for nice clothing? Are you much more comfortable today than your ancestors were in the old country?

Now here's a completely different way of looking at the phrase "Thank you to the One who provides clothes for the naked." For a moment, let's go deeper and explore whether this daily phrase of thankfulness is about much more than just our personal clothing.

One of the many rabbinic interpretations of "Thank you to the One who provides clothes for the naked" is that it makes us mindful of the fact that we are in a sometimes-compassionate world where there are all sorts of good people (you might be one of them) who are consistently doing helpful things to make sure that vulnerable people have dignity and important opportunities even if they don't have very many bucks in their pocket or any savings.

When I stop for a moment and say, "Thank you for providing clothes for the naked," I think of the Jewish-based flow of compassion that is found at places like the inexpensive thrift stores of the National Council of Jewish Women. Think about it for just a second: when you or I donate used clothes, cash, or other items to the NCJW, we not only make it possible for someone who is impoverished or out of work to be able to afford a very inexpensive but nicely tailored job interview outfit (so they can show up with confidence that they aren't going to be rejected because of appearance). We also make it possible for low-income families to be able to clothe their kids for school, so the kids won't be teased or shunned by classmates on the playground for not having stylish clothes. We also become part of an ongoing flow of lovingkindness because the NCJW thrift stores set aside money from the sale of used clothes and other items for the funding of support groups, phone hot lines, and seminars for women who want to escape from abusive partners or violent home situations.

On a stressful morning when I see in the news headlines that people are mistreating one another near and far, I can stop for a moment and say, "Blessed is the One that is continually creating a world where there are also generous people and generous organizations that are trying to clothe, protect, and assist people who have felt unprotected, vulnerable, or naked." Knowing that we are in partnership with the Divine Presence to clothe the vulnerable members of this world makes me want to stay healthy, active, and involved in order to be a part of that enormous global team of compassion and repair—the ones who clothe the vulnerable.

Another possible way of interpreting "Blessed is the Eternal One, our God, who provides clothing for the naked" is the belief among many traditional and observant Jews that we human beings are somewhat naked (and easily led astray) until we are "clothed" in the teachings of the Torah on how to live each day by doing justly, loving mercy, and to walk humbly with the Creator of All That Exists.

In your own life, have you ever felt "unprotected" or "susceptible" in the presence of a charismatic or highly-manipulative individual who tried to talk you into something--using flowery words or lavish enticements? What kept you from being permanently swept under by this person's charm? Were there some deep values, or important teachings, or supportive people who helped you stay somewhat centered even when this person was trying to sway you?

So when you or I take a few seconds in the morning to say, "Thank you to the One who provides clothing for the naked," we have a quick chance to be grateful for some of the teachers, friends, books, counseling, conversations, and debates that have kept us strong and centered. We can take a brief moment to say thank you for the specific people who cared about us and helped us to be "clothed" in the ways of doing good and living a compassionate, healthy life.

You might have your own unique and personal way of interpreting, "I am thankful to the One who provides clothing for the naked." For instance, have you ever been in a situation where you saw a homeless person, or a person with a severe mental illness, who was agitated in a public place or along the sidewalk and either you or some other angel of the Divine provided that person with food, clothing, or opportunities for shelter. Or did you ever find yourself in a situation where someone with Alzheimer's, Dementia, or another serious ailment was unable to dress, bathe, or clean oneself (and you or some other compassionate person did the holy work of providing clothing and protection for that vulnerable soul).

When you take a moment each morning to feel thankful that there are people, organizations, spiritual teachings, and open hearts in this world who deeply desire to provide clothing and protection to those who are vulnerable, it can boost your energy (even on a horrific news day) for being of service and doing something useful in your corner of the world. In just a few seconds, these morning blessings are about rising above the coldness of the world so that we can appreciate the warm flows of energy that we can tap into and feel boosted by. As Michelle Obama has suggested many times, "When they go low, we go high."

A Quick Few Words that Can Also Prevent a Lot of Pain and Trouble

Here's one more of the traditional morning blessings that sounds at first like no big deal, but in fact it's a fascinating, uplifting, very-big-deal that can boost your energy for the day in front of you.

One of the Hebrew phrases in the morning blessings that many people tend to rush through all over the world are: Bah-rukh Atah Adonai (or HaShem or Yud Hei Vov Hei) Eloheinu Melekh Ha-Olam Ha-May-Kheen Mitz-ah-day Gah-vehr.

In English it usually gets translated, "Blessed are You, Eternal One our God, who makes firm each person's steps."

On a surface level, it seems to be about walking with firm steps, rather than clumsy steps. Why would that be a morning blessing that Jews have recited daily for many centuries?

I have found that at some synagogues and Jewish temples throughout the United States and elsewhere, there is a relatively new practice in which the warm and inclusive rabbi asks congregants in the middle of the morning blessings to consider for a moment, "Which one of these phrases speaks to you personally this morning and touches your soul?" At various Jewish congregations when I've been asked to be a guest speaker visiting for the first time, I've heard people respond to the rabbi's intriguing question by standing up and expressing some wonderful interpretations of the seemingly no-big-deal "Thank you to the One who makes firm each person's steps."

Here are a few possibilities from several parts of the world for you to consider if you want to say this quick morning blessing with a deeper intention or a more personal, inspiring meaning:

- a woman who recently recovered from knee surgery (and weeks of intense physical therapy exercises) stood up at her congregation and said, "I used to take sidewalks and stairs for granted. But now since my knee ordeal, I love this morning blessing because it reminds me how exquisite it is to be able to walk again and how mindful I need to be whenever I'm dealing with cracked, uneven sidewalks or narrow, slippery stairs that require holding onto the railing. I feel like this short, quick daily reminder to be grateful for each firm step is a wake-up call that says, 'Walk with careful wisdom and be thankful for each moment of being able to move through life gracefully and joyfully.' Our ability to walk can get disrupted in a millisecond, so please stay conscious of how precious it is to be able to walk safely."

- a man who has been studying Jewish spirituality for many years stood up at his congregation and said that this daily one-line prayer of gratitude to "the One who makes firm each person's steps" reminds him each morning of the teachings of the Baal Shem Tov (the founder of the Hasidic movement), who said that if you walk each day with greater awareness of nature, trees, and profound spiritual teachings about the Creator of All That Exists, your steps will be joyful and solid, rather than clumsy and misdirected. This man explained, "Sometimes when I'm taking my morning walk and I see the trees, the sky, and the clouds, I feel so fortunate to be able to breathe deeply and say, 'Thank you for each small step, HaShem, that You are helping me make in this lifetime. Each conscious step makes me more aware of the beauty of Your creation.'"

- a woman who has been involved in Twelve-Step programs stood up at her synagogue and said, "When I say thank you to the One who makes firm each person's steps," I think of the sponsors, the helpful friends, the supportive loved ones, the inspiring meetings, and the daily tools that have kept me on track one day at a time as I've worked the steps of repairing my shaky life that now has much better balance and stability. I need to remind myself at least once a day that I am walking through life more successfully now because of the spiritual tools and allies that have helped me to stay firmly on a more mindful path."

- a gender non-binary individual I met at a Jewish prayer service (where the rabbi asked congregants to consider which of the blessings felt especially meaningful on that particular day) stood up and said, "When I stop for a moment each morning and I say thank you to the One who makes firm each person's steps, I feel grateful that each day, one small step at a time, I am discovering and getting closer to the truth about the genuine, unique soul I have been given by God. I used to feel wobbly, unsteady, and somewhat unsafe going out into the world, but now, thankfully, I can walk with authenticity and live much closer to what God created inside my soul."

- a man who had recently lost his wife in a tragic car accident stood up and said to his congregation, "I used to just race through the words 'Blessed is the One who makes firm each person's steps.' But now I feel like I'm slowly recovering from the sadness and the emptiness I was feeling for many months and I'm beginning to be able to move forward again with firmness and support. I am grateful for each step I am taking to heal and to regain my footing in life."

As you say silently or out loud the words, "Blessed are You, Eternal One our God, who makes firm each person's steps," what specific step forward or what exact need for firm, mindful steps come to mind for you personally? Do you feel guided or supported to stay balanced and on track? Or do you feel shaky or close to losing your way? Reminding yourself daily in a quick, sincere moment of alertness to look around and see what can help you make firm your steps today can be enormously helpful. Feel free to make this quick phrase come alive in your own words so that your body, mind, and spirit can move through your day with greater safety, teamwork, and joy.

Overcoming the Grogginess and Fogginess at Other Times of the Day

Sometimes even on a day when the morning starts with a centering method and a good burst of energy and clarity, there will be moments at 11am, or Noon, or 3pm, or 5pm, or 7pm when your energy drops and your brain feels overloaded or consumed by worries or frustrations. I know from my counseling clients, my family members, and from my own life, that sometimes it's not easy to make the shift from tiredness to gratitude in the middle of a stressful day or a tense moment.

So in Judaism there are gentle reminders placed throughout the day, the week, the month, and the year that say essentially, "Yes, it's really frustrating sometimes and yet there are still some things that you can honestly feel thankful about and that can give you a much-needed boost in the middle of a difficult situation."

Some Jewish teachings suggest that if you say one-hundred blessings (or honest thank you statements) each day, your soul will be more nourished and vibrant. Other Jewish teachings talk about thirty-six blessings or quick thank you statements per day. Still other Jewish teachers recommend ten blessings or brief thank you moments each day. Many Jewish teachers and writers simply focus on the holy act of saying one sincere and uplifting thank you (even if it's just for the smallest, most ordinary thing) and how that one short moment of gratitude can shift the brain and the physical body from tiredness to renewed good energy.

Here's a quick example of how to get boosted by this "even the smallest, most ordinary thing," especially on days when you are feeling tired, distracted, or agitated. For eighteen years, I've been in a 9 a.m. Mussar (Jewish ethics and personal growth) study group on Saturday mornings with Rabbi Miriam Hamrell where she starts each weekly discussion by asking us to close our eyes for a moment and savor one small, sweet memory of something good that we experienced already in the past few hours with any of our five senses. It might be the taste of a delicious cup of coffee, tea, juice, or water. It could be a flower, a tree, a bird call, or the rush of the wind, or the feeling of the sun's rays on our faces. Or the eyes or the smile of someone we care about, or their voice on the phone, or the words of affection, support, or humor that we had most recently with someone. Or a moment of kindness or goodness that we witnessed recently.

Rabbi Miriam then asks us to bring that sweet memory to mind every so often during the next several hours or days so that we can deliberately bathe our souls in gratitude whenever we are feeling depleted or distracted. Then we breathe calmly in and out as we say thank you for even the smallest moments of goodness we are noticing right now (fully aware that there might be things that are difficult or in need of improvement, but from a place of gratitude we will have more energy and creativity to deal with the tough moments).

If you are willing to stop for just a few seconds right at this precise moment, ask yourself, "What is one sweet memory of something I experienced with any of my five senses that I enjoyed today or this week (and that I probably have started to forget or take for granted already, but right now I can bring it back to mind and bathe my soul and renew my positive energy with it)?" You and I have the ability at any time of day (late morning, early afternoon, late afternoon, early evening) to bring back good memories and sweet moments, even though our problem-seeking brains are racing to find something worrisome or unresolved (but for this brief conscious moment we are focusing on what is sweet and positive so that we can boost our energy to deal more effectively with whatever is on our plates).

If you or any of your loved ones have a long history of anxiety or worrying, please don't feel rushed or pressured to change instantaneously. I realize we can't force anyone else or ourselves to stop obsessing on what's broken, or to insist, "No more worrying from now on." In fact, opening up to thankfulness has to come from an act of free will and for many people it needs to happen gradually, not all at once. You might have noticed already that if you say to someone in a harsh, impatient, or shaming tone of voice, "Count your blessings, for crying out loud," the unspoken response will usually be, "Back off, bossy one! Get out of my face. Don't tell me to count my blessings. Can't you see I'm having a tough time right now."

But in Judaism, it's not a scolding voice or an impatient, bossy attitude that asks gently, "Is there one thing or a few things you can notice right now for a few seconds in order to bathe your weary soul with thankfulness or resilience?" Rather, it's a thoughtful, compassionate voice that comes from love and genuine care for your neshamah, your pure soul that needs a boost every so often to emerge from tiredness into a renewed sense of gratitude and forward momentum.

My goal in writing this chapter on Jewish blessings and daily resilience is not to boss you around or to insist that you must say anything you don't want to say. I'm just offering you the option of trying out (when you are ready) the possibility of outsmarting the anxious brain we all have. I'm giving you a few ingredients for an experiment you can do on your own when you have a free moment--that if you decide to say one thank you a day, or a few thank you statements a day, or eventually a few more than that—to try out this personal experiment and notice whether or not it makes a difference in whether you feel less tired and more energized. My hope is that each time you boost your own resilience and clarity by shifting your mood from debilitating tiredness to uplifting gratitude, your life (and the life of those you are caring about on a daily basis) will be enormously enhanced. I strongly believe that moments of thankfulness are like inexpensive, easy-to-use batteries that can re-charge our souls.

CHAPTER THREE:

Would You Like to Experience "a Great Love" More Often?

Imagine for a moment that a truly wonderful, compassionate individual has been consistently and respectfully loving you and sending you gifts, but you were unaware of how this love and these gifts originated. Also, imagine for a few seconds that this amazing source of love and generosity has been longing for your love in return, but you had no clue how much this intensely-devoted someone desires your love.

In this chapter, we are going to be talking about love and mutuality in relationships. It's quite possible that by the end of this chapter, you might be in the mood to write some love notes or sing some love songs that sound a lot like, "I hope you don't mind, I hope you don't mind, that I put down in words, how wonderful life is while you're in the world." Even if you are a somewhat skeptical or justifiably cautious human being, are you slightly interested in experiencing such an intense and joyful feeling of love?

We will also be discussing in this chapter two very profound and energizing prayers that talk about love (one from the evening prayer book for weekdays, holidays, and Sabbaths, along with one from the morning prayer book that gets sung or spoken on weekdays, holidays, and Sabbaths). I am hoping that these two remarkable prayers will come alive for you like never before and that your heart and mind will be opened up by the possibility of such an intense, ongoing love relationship happening in your own life now and in the future.

The Rabbi Who Dared to Talk About "Love" in Public

Several years ago, I attended a High Holiday service where the some-what-large congregation was led by Rabbi Debra Orenstein, who comes from several generations of rabbis and whose books on femi-nist Jewish perspectives (including "Lifecycles 1: Jewish Women on Life Passages and Personal Milestones") have inspired large num-bers of people worldwide.

During her High Holiday sermon that year, Rabbi Orenstein announced, "I want to talk today about a topic that you very rarely hear contemporary rabbis say out loud in a synagogue because we don't want to sound like a huckstering minister on cable television. I want to talk about whether in Judaism there is a sense that God loves you, or whether that's no longer what most Jews believe, espe-cially after the Holocaust."

I could see lots of people squirming in their seats. This was clear-ly a topic you don't usually hear about in a progressive, sophisticated modern gathering of somewhat-skeptical Jews. I think people were wondering, "What the heck is she going to say about 'does God love you' that wouldn't sound hokey or questionable?"

That day, Rabbi Orenstein spoke honestly and passionately about how Judaism has always (even today) had specific ways of experi-encing God's love and how to feel connected each day to a Loving Presence without abandoning your rational brain or your desire to be realistic and sensible in today's world. I am grateful to her for addressing this important topic of "is it reasonable to feel connected to an infinite Source of Compassion and Love, even when there is so much cruelty and injustice that still needs to be confronted in this world."

Now, before I describe the Jewish concept of "the Great Love," let me ask for your honest reaction so far:

- Do you feel a bit skeptical or hesitant to be engaging in a conversation about "Does God love us" or even more personally "Does God love you the individual?"

- Or are you slightly curious about whether it's possible to believe sensibly during the 21st century about a divine flow of love and nurturance (that maybe was never explained to you in a believable manner up until now)?

Here for you to consider (and possibly be inspired or energized by) are four, briefly-described Jewish versions of what it means to connect with "the Great Love" that is available if we open up to it:

Indication #1 of a Great Love: The Abundant Web and Womb of Nourishment that You and I Didn't Create, But that We Benefit from Daily

In every morning prayer service on weekdays, holidays, and the Sabbath, there is a beautiful melody and poem called "Ahavah Rabbah" (the word Ahavah means "love" and the word Rabbah means "great, abundant, or everlasting") that has been sung or spoken for close to 2,000 years.

One of the words that gets repeated several times in that prayer-poem is Rakhamim, which is a fascinating Hebrew word (and if you explore the deeper meanings of the word Rakhamim you will begin to have an important clue about what "the Great Love" is all about).

The closely-related words Rakhamim, Ha-rakh-amahn, Hahm-rakhaim, and Rakhaim (that you will find right next to each other in the first paragraph of the Ahavah Rabbah prayer-poem) not only mean "compassion" or "merciful," but they come from the root word "Rekhem" which means "womb."

I've always found that fascinating—that the Hebrew word for compassion and mercy is also simultaneously a three-dimensional sense of a nurturing "womb" that gives us bursts of life-sustaining energy and guidance. Picture that for a few seconds—that you and I are breathing smoothly right now (I hope), and we are definitely alive right at this moment (I hope), because we are fortunate enough to live in a nurturing "womb" of oxygen, gravity, sunlight, breezes, shady trees, morning dew, delicious foods, vitamins, minerals, and supportive individuals who make it possible for us to be who we are.

In other words, when you say or sing the "Ahavah Rabbah" poem-prayer, you are connecting yourself to an appreciation that there is a life-giving Source that provides many forms of nurturance, support, and energy to us each day. For example, right now as you are looking at this page and these words, there are thousands of microscopic nutrients flowing through your body from the meals you've eaten in the past 24 hours and these nutrients come from an abundant Source that includes the sunlight you and I didn't create, the chemical reactions in the soil that you and I barely understand, plus herbs, vitamins, minerals, solids, and fluids in the nutritious foods we eat that energize us, like a "womb of life" that is continually supporting a growing, vulnerable being (even when we are asleep).

When a Jewish person says or sings "Rakhamim" or "Ha-rakh-amahn" or "Hahm-rakhaim" or "Rakhaim" (the words for "compassion" and "womb" mentioned in the prayer-poem Ahavah Rabbah, the Great Love), it's somewhat like a Native American chanting thanks to Mother Earth for the flow of nutrition, sunlight, rains, dew, and healing that surround and connect all of us. We Jews might not dress or dance exactly like Native Americans, but we have a very similar sense of connecting through chanting and song to the nurturing web of life that sustains us so generously.

Even if you've always rushed through these words in the past, or not been aware of what they mean, consider for a moment that saying the Hebrew word for "compassion" and "womb," which is Rakhamim, is a possible wake-up call that can remind us that we are definitely on the receiving end of a generous flow of gifts and life-sustaining basics that we often take for granted. Without those daily gifts of warm sunlight, fertile soil, much-needed moisture, hard-working farm employees, and nutritious vitamins and minerals in the food we eat (all of which come from an abundant universe that surrounds us and assists us), we might not be able to stay alive very long or be able to say, "Thank you Rakhamim, the compassionate womb of life-sustaining elements, for loving and supporting us day after day after day."

Here's something to try out and experiment with: The next time you are saying a prayer in private or at a congregational prayer service that mentions God's love or compassion, make sure to stop for a conscious moment and let yourself feel surrounded by a brilliantly-created "womb" of nurturing elements that come from an abundant and hard-to-define Creative Source. Then you will be able to sing out and say with honesty, "Yes, we are truly cared for and loved by an extremely abundant love." Not only does it feel uplifting and joyful to celebrate your connection to the abundant Source of Life, but it also inspires us to take good care of the delicate womb (the Earth, the waters, the Earth's atmosphere) in which we are living each day with vulnerable interdependence and increasing fragility.

Indication #2 of a Great Love: The Instruction Guides that Can Help Us Respond to People and Situations Each Day with More Compassion and Decency

A second and equally-important flow of love and support that we can open up to in order to help us in our daily lives are the wise teachings that get passed from generation to generation about how to treat one another with dignity and how to live with integrity, resilience, and purpose. In several Jewish prayers where the word "love, ahavah" is mentioned, the deeper meaning is that when we learn something useful from a caring person or when we teach something useful to someone we care about, we are part of a remarkable chain of loving guidance that aligns us with the Nourishing Breath of Life.

In your own personal experience, as you think about the various "Life Insight Moments" that you have received thus far during your time on Earth on how to become a more compassionate, patient, resilient, and decent human being, are there some vivid memories that come to mind from when you were lovingly guided by any or all of the following:

- Are there some specific words, conversations, or stories that a Jewish teacher, a Jewish relative, a Jewish writer, or a Jewish friend or role model have given you that helped you improve some challenging area of your life?

- Is there a particular rabbi, cantor, teacher, counselor, friend, family member, or colleague who truly listened to you during a tough moment in your life and helped you explore options on how to turn a difficult situation into a renewed sense of hope, creativity, connection, or purpose?

- Is there at least one person in your life so far who had a deep love for Jewish study or Jewish wisdom, and you felt fortunate to be having a thoughtful and meaningful conversation with that caring individual?

I remember as a teenager having several private conversations with a very patient and wise rabbi in my hometown of Detroit who was willing to listen calmly to my questions, concerns, and points of disagreement. More than anything else, this rabbi taught me that when two or more Jews are discussing something holy or complicated, it is a conversation based in love and mutual respect, rather than a conversation of one-upmanship or clashing egos.

As you think about your own personal experiences when you have been learning about Judaism, learning about how to live a meaningful life, and learning how to respond to specific difficult situations with decency and compassion, you might also have had some genuine moments of being guided with love and patience by a very compassionate and open-hearted teacher, friend, or family member who knew the importance of transmitting holy wisdom with caring and mutual respect. If so, then you know from direct personal experience what is being said in the Jewish prayers that mention "love, ahavah" as the way we are intended to learn and to teach as Jews. In order to guide someone on how to live a compassionate, meaningful life, it kinda makes sense for both the teacher and the student (or for the study partners) to be treating each other with patience and kindness.

On the other hand, if you have had some judgmental or harsh instructors, colleagues, or family members who didn't live up to that essential Jewish teaching "to engage lovingly in study and to listen deeply to the unique wisdom of each precious soul who asks a question or offers a differing perspective," I am so sorry for the discomfort or the frustrations you have had in the past. It is very sad when someone with a swollen ego or a lot of book learning (but not a lot of heart learning) talks to a questioning student, family member, or colleague in a harsh or insensitive way. I hope the next time you sing or say the joyful words of the morning prayer "Ahavah Rabbah, the great love," or the evening prayer "Ahavat Olam, the everlasting love," that you will open up your own heart to the possibility that now and in the future, you will be able steer clear of harsh, unloving "know-it-alls" and seek out those who are patient, kind, humble and much more respectful of who you are as a unique individual.

There is so much to learn each week and each year about how to be a good person (especially about how to be patient and compassionate during very stressful moments when you're feeling edgy) and how to deal with all the challenges in our lives and in our world. Please make sure to surround yourself with loving souls and compassionate teachers who can help each of us to keep learning, keep growing, and keep being involved in the repair of our fragile selves and our fragile world. Then you will know from your own direct experience what it means to sing or say, "Thank You for this Great Love, this flow of learning and guidance that has helped us stay centered, compassionate, and resilient through all sorts of challenging moments."

Indication #3 of a Great Love: The Possibility of "Relationship Repair" If You Have Felt Estranged from the Creative Source

Now it's time to talk about the sense of estrangement or "falling out of love" that many Jews have felt toward God or religion. As any couples' therapist can tell you, it takes a passionate difference of opinion (and a passionate desire to reconnect) in order for a relationship to deepen and endure. The couples who know that it's normal for there to be occasional misunderstandings or hurt feelings, and then a mutual effort to listen with an open heart to one another and repair the sense of distance, are the couples who have the most profound and long-lasting partnerships.

The same is true in our relationship with the mysterious Source of Life that is beyond human description. In Judaism, one of the ways to "love God" is that it is permissible to wrestle and disagree with God—it's an essential part of being in a genuine, two-way loving relationship. Many of the most respected Jews in the Torah (Abraham, Sarah, Jacob, Moses, Miriam, Hannah, David) have moments of being upset with God, for speaking honestly from the heart, and for (sooner or later) repairing those feelings of disagreement or estrangement.

In your own relationship with God or religion, have there been some ups and downs and disagreements? If so, you can rest assured that it's a normal part of being in a genuine "sometimes smooth, sometimes rocky" relationship (that might need an occasional conversation about how to repair the distance between you). The authentic "sometimes we argue and yet we find a way to hear each other and feel connected again" relationship between Jews and the Source of Life has been written about in many books, including "Arguing with God: A Jewish Tradition" by Rabbi Anson Laytner and "For Those Who Can't Believe" by Rabbi Harold Schulweis. Both of these authors see the moments of belief and the moments of doubt as being essential elements in a true, honest relationship.

I remember in 1997 when my publisher sent me on a tour of the Southern United States for one of my earlier books (on diverse ways to understand the Ten Utterances or The Ten Commandments), numerous people from other religions came up to me after each speech and asked in a very hushed, anxious voice, "Is it really allowed for Jews to wrestle and disagree with God or the most traditional writings? Do you Jews really do that kind of questioning in front of your family members, or in a public forum in front of a clergy member? I could never do that in the tradition I was raised with!"

Each time I would hear the anxiety and hesitation in their voices, I realized that the encouragement we have been given in Judaism to ask deep questions is not something that is encouraged in every spiritual tradition. As you think about what it means in your own life to be a Jewish person who has permission to argue and converse intimately and lovingly with a mysterious Source of Life, you might recall Tevye in "Fiddler on the Roof" walking along the unpaved road and having deep, intense and loving conversations with God (like you would with a wise and caring best friend). Each time Tevye encounters another tough situation in his daily life where he is being challenged to learn, to grow, and to expand beyond his comfort zone, he opens up his heart to the ever-present Source of Compassion and he says it exactly how it is—with true emotion and authentic longing.

So if you or someone you love have felt abandoned by God, upset with God, distant from God, or unsure about God, please know that in Judaism you are invited to tell the truth about your complicated relationship (or even the painful moments of "falling out of love" and your efforts to repair the connection) with the Eternal One. Especially in the current era, when millions of Jews have felt a bit distant or unsure about "where was God during the Holocaust," the need for relationship repair is more urgent than ever before.

Here's a gentle question to consider if you want to take a step toward "relationship repair:"

Are you a little bit distant from God or religion because of what happened during the Holocaust or during other times more recently when horrible things happened to innocent people?

I don't have all the answers. But I do know (as a couples' therapist and as someone who has studied for many years the question of "what can we believe after the Holocaust") that it's quite possible to reconnect with the Divine Presence and start to repair that deeply personal relationship if you consider some of the following explanations of "where was God during a particular tragedy or a horrific moment?"

Right now, as a gentle step toward addressing some of the distance or feelings of distrust that you or someone else might be feeling toward God or the Creative Source, let's start by looking at the evidence and bring in a few eye-witnesses:

Please consider as a first eye-witness on the question of "Can we still believe that there is a God that listens and cares, and is it reasonable to feel love toward that hard-to-define sense of Divine Presence," I would like to invite you to hear from Elie Wiesel, the Nobel Prize winning author, activist, and passionate soul who barely survived the Holocaust. Elie Wiesel wrote a play about putting God on trial, went through decades of arguing with God and wrestling with questions of faith, and also wrote a fascinating and widely-published newspaper article one September on Yom Kippur that said:

"Master of the Universe, let us make up. It is time. How long can we go on being angry? After all, Auschwitz was not something that came down ready-made from heaven. It was conceived by men, implemented by men, staffed by men. And their sin was not only to destroy us, but their attempt to destroy You as well."

He continues, "Ought we not to think of your pain, too? Watching your children suffer at the hands of your other children haven't you also suffered? Let us make up, Master of the Universe, in spite of everything that happened. It is unbearable to be divorced from you this long."

Wiesel is asking, "Why are we blaming and distancing ourselves from the Compassionate Source, when in fact the cruelty was cooked up by a specific group of hateful humans? Why are we cutting off from the Divine Presence, when in fact it was some broken and gullible human beings acting against God's ways that caused the enormous harm?"

If you or someone you care about has felt betrayed or ignored by God, it may take a long time for that broken trust to begin to heal. It's not easy to start trusting and connecting again. My hope is that you or this person you know who is feeling betrayed by God will consider taking at least a first step of exploring with someone who is a good listener to hear your honest truth about what you have experienced and the doubts it stirred up in you.

Now, there is a second group of witnesses I'd like you to hear from who have something to say about the "relationship repair" that is possible between humans and the Source of Life. Specifically, there are numerous Jewish writers and scholars who have suggested that the Creator of the World doesn't control or intervene 100% of the time, but rather this Source of Life intentionally made room in the amazing, vast creation for there to be human free will, some randomness, and some imperfections that need to be repaired. The natural world of earthquakes, tornadoes, hurricanes, mosquitos, and viruses do what they do based on a dynamic flexibility and a randomness that is hardwired into most natural phenomena. If it weren't for that randomness and for humans to have free will over major portions of their own lives, this would be a boring, inflexible, totally-predictable world with no genuine choice-making and no surprises.

If you think about it, our world definitely has been designed with lots of room for human trial-and-error learning where we sometimes mess things up at first, or do some cruel and horrible things for a while, until we own up to our part in the on-going stewardship and repair of the planet. Like a parent who gives the car keys to an impulsive teen driver, the Source of Life has given humans a lot of license to do a wide variety of unpredictable and risky things that would make a parent or a Creator cringe and wonder, "What was I thinking? Why did I let this impulsive and self-centered person have so much free will and so much free reign to do so many questionable things?" (It should also be noted that we humans also have a lot of free will to do compassionate, creative, and wonderful things—in fact, many people in the middle of a horrific situation or when they see injustice or cruelty, they remember to ask the Creative Source for strength and wisdom to help generate innovative ways to do the right thing and to be the earthly partners of the Creative Source in repairing what's clearly broken).

So if you stop for a moment and think carefully about the question "Should we blame God for the Holocaust in a world that has lots of unpredictable human choice-making and built-in natural randomness," the logical answer is that there were millions of people throughout the world who were deeply listening to "the still small voice within" (one of the many names for God) and who wanted to stop the Nazis and their enablers from their destructive ways. But there were also a number of extremely unhelpful people in the U.S. State Department, the Immigration Department, and the Congress who (either because of their own anti-Semitism or just their indifference to the plight of the Jews) refused to increase the restrictive quotas on how many people could enter American soil, or to allow the United States military to blow up the train tracks that were carrying innocent Jewish souls and others to the concentration camps. There were also a number of extremely unhelpful people in the British government who (either because of their own anti-Semitism or just their indifference to the plight of the Jews) refused to allow more Jews to enter British-controlled Palestine, which would have saved many, many thousands of lives.

Rather than blaming God for what specific humans in positions of power were doing, is it possible that the Compassionate Source of Life was sending messages that many people felt in their hearts, but that certain unhelpful individuals in power were refusing to hear? Is it possible that the still small voice of God was never silenced, absent, or abandoning us, but that specific humans chose not to listen (and for a painfully long while those closed-hearted forces were creating terrible horrors)?

I can't tell you what to believe or whether to believe. But I can tell you that it's quite okay to have moments of questioning, arguing, wrestling, listening, forgiving, and renewing with the One that is beyond human words. Please know that on any given day the personal relationship you have with the ever-flowing Source of Life can shift back and forth between deep connection and feelings of distance.

In other words, the next time you sing or say the words of "Ahavah Rabbah, the great love" or "Ahavat Olam, the everlasting love," please check in with your own exquisite heart and ask yourself, "Am I open right now to a renewed, warm connection and a re-awakening of the feelings of love I have been holding back? Or am I still carrying a grudge or a cold resentment from the past?" To experience a "Great Love," you sometimes need to admit to yourself or to a supportive counselor or advisor, "I have been wrestling with some doubts. This complicated love relationship is going to require some work and some healing in order to feel strengthened and very connected again."

Indication #4 of a Great Love: The Feelings of Awe that We Sometimes Put in Writing or Speak from the Heart

Here is a fourth and final way to experience a sense of the "Great Love" that might energize your daily life in new and inspiring ways:

Have you ever written a love note, a poem, or a tender message of appreciation or deep longing to someone you adored? Have you ever spoken (in an intimate whisper or out loud) words of endearment to someone whose very essence made you feel quite alive? Have you ever written a note, a journal entry, or a song to someone you miss and wish you could be close with again?

On a busy day or during a stressful week, you might be thinking, "I have absolutely no energy right now to be writing a love note or saying tender words of appreciation or longing to a loved one. Right now, I'm just trying to check off the things on my 'To Do' list and I'm feeling very behind schedule."

That's why it's so radical, bold, and healing to stop for a few seconds in the middle of a frenetic day and give yourself a moment of loving connection between your individual soul and the Soul of the Universe. It's as if you suddenly have the superpower of being able to rise above the tensions of the day and embrace the big picture—that we are complicated beings who have a lot of love in us and we are possibly here on Earth to do acts of lovingkindness as partners with the Creative Breath of Life.

Are you willing to tap into that deep well of caring and tenderness for at least a few seconds in the next few minutes, or hours, or days? Are you willing to have a real-life openness to let yourself experience "a Great Love?"

In practical, realistic terms, here are a few ways you can reconnect with profound feelings of love, even on a busy day or during a stressful week. See which one of these options feels most like who you are and what you are comfortable doing in the next few minutes, or during the next few hours, or possibly in the next few days:

- Option A for Connecting with Words of Love: Rather than struggling to find the right words to express how you feel in perfectly eloquent phrases, just pick one of your favorite love songs and imagine saying it with genuine honesty from your individual soul to the mysterious Soul of the Universe.

For example, there is a well-known song by Paul McCartney called "Maybe I'm Amazed" that has the sense of awe and appreciation a caring person feels when we stop and realize that someone is helping us, or guiding us, or boosting our strength. With passion and vulnerability, the sensitive songwriter from Liverpool admits, "Maybe I'm amazed at the way you help me sing my song, right me when I'm wrong. Maybe I'm amazed at the way I really need you."

Have you ever admitted to yourself or to someone else that you are vulnerable and that you need someone's help and inspiration during a tough time in your life? Have you ever thought to yourself or said to someone else, "I try to be so self-reliant and very independent, but sometimes I have to admit that I do need some love and support to get me through these difficult days and nights. It amazes me that I'm willing to break out of my protective shell and that I'm allowing someone into my heart and my life more than I have previously."

Obviously, McCartney's "Maybe I'm Amazed" was written for a specific person. But what if you were saying to the Breath-of-Life or to the Source-of-Creativity-and-Deep-Wisdom, "It's hard for me to admit this, but I do depend on You and I love when I feel guided by You." Or if you were to say to the One that breathes life into you, "I guess I don't say this too often, but maybe I'm amazed at the way I really need You."

For just a moment, say those words to the One That Is Beyond Words and see what it feels like to admit, "Maybe I'm amazed at the way you help me sing my song, right me when I'm wrong. Maybe I'm amazed at the way I really need You."

On the other hand, there might also be a part of your brain that is saying, "Hey, wait a minute, I'm still not 100% sure about this thing called love." For millions of people, it feels much too vulnerable and a little too raw to just come out and sing "I'm amazed by You" or "I love You" or "I need You" to a mysterious life force that we can't quite describe in human words.

If skepticism or uncertainty feels more honest for you when it comes to expressing love or connection to a Source of Life, then possibly a more cautious, careful phrase would be more genuine and accurate for you at this moment. It could be something that has curiosity in it, but also a lot of hesitance or uncertainty--a bit like the Taylor Swift song "Delicate" in which she says about whether it's safe or not to open up her heart, "Is it too soon to do this yet? Is it chill that you're in my head? Cuz I know that it's del-i-cate" (and the fragile echo-voice in her song repeats the hesitant word "del-i-cate").

Have you ever felt a little too vulnerable, a little too unsure, or a little too cautious about expressing your love or your gratitude to a Source that you are not 100% sure is even there? Is your love song to the Ever-flowing Breath of Life more like an honest question, "Can I really call out to You when I'm in a tough place?"

Whichever "true-to-who-you-are" lyrics of love, or longing, or uncertainty that you choose to experiment with, please take a moment and see how it feels to be saying words that open you up to a stream of connection and warmth between you as an individual and the mysterious Breath of Life that fills the entire universe. Notice whether your words (written by someone else) have some uncertainty, some intense belief or curiosity, or some joy and connection to be saying to the mysterious Divine Presence, "I am starting to have the glimmer of feelings of love for You. I'm a little uncomfortable and awkward saying these things to You. But why not? I'm just going to say it!"

- Option B for Connecting with Words of Love. Finding the words that feel true to you by looking at various prayers or phrases in a Jewish prayer book.

Quite often there are passionate words, poetry, and songs that someone else has already written and their artistry stirs up your own connection to a sense of love and curiosity toward the mysterious One-That-Is-and-Will-Always-Be. Here's what you can do today or this week to find the words that speak to your soul: For just a few quick minutes as a much-needed relief from all the distractions of life, you can look through a Jewish prayer book or one of your favorite books on Jewish spirituality and choose one specific phrase that you personally find moving or inspiring for expressing your particular form of love and connection with the Creative Source.

It might be a line from a Psalm where David is skeptical or anxious at first and then feels deeply nourished by his connection to a Presence that lifts him up. It might be a line from a modern feminist writer who connects with the In-Dwelling Presence (the Shekhinah), or the beauty of nature, or the vast Fountain of Blessings, in a way that feels true and inspiring for you today. It might be a line in the prayer book that you rushed through in the past, but right now when you explore it with new eyes and new curiosity, you begin to feel the intense longing and connection that is underneath the words.

Now when you say that same phrase at services or in the privacy of your own home, imagine for a few seconds that your individual soul is raising up feelings of love and awe to the One who has created so much beauty, wisdom, and diversity in this world. In most Jewish prayer books in the 21st century, we are being given lots of choices and lots of different variations. Today there is much more recognition in Judaism that your unique, personal way of feeling a love and connection to the Source of Life and Wisdom is a bit different from how your grandpa or your grandma expressed their particular feelings of love and connection.

Here's one option to consider on how to make a standard phrase from the prayer book come alive for you: One of my favorite quick lines to sing when I feel like offering up love to the mysterious Source of Compassion is the energizing phrase from Psalm 150 that gets sung or said at many morning services on weekdays, holidays, and the Sabbath.

The final line of Psalm 150 in most prayer books says simply, "Kol ha-neshahmah t'hah-leil Yah." Quickly, here are some translations: Kol means every or all. Ha-neshahmah means the soul, essence, or breathing life force of someone. T'hah-leil means to praise, honor, celebrate, or express appreciation. The Hebrew word "Yah" is a fascinating multi-leveled word that can simultaneously mean "breath" or "soul" or "God."

Now if you put these four words together in a meaningful way, this uplifting phrase "Kol ha-neshahmah t'hah-leil Yah" can be translated as "Everything that has breath is praising or celebrating You, the Breath of Life," or "Every soul is expressing in their own unique way one aspect of the amazing, vast Soul of the Universe," or "Every breath from inside me is lifting up toward honoring You."

Or if you are a visual person, you can connect more deeply with this phrase "Everything that has breath is celebrating Your Ongoing Creation" by imagining that every flowering plant in a garden (or every Joshua tree in the desert) is rising up toward the sky, or that every diverse human waking up today is doing their part in the ever-flowing completion of the world.

Or you can come up with your own individual way of visualizing that all the souls of the world, all the people and things that are breathing and alive, are right now expressing their soul-essence in millions of different ways as you say or sing, "Kol ha-neshahmah t'hah-leil Yah...everything that has breath is an expression of You, the Breath of Life, the Vast Soul of the Universe."

What an amazing four-word prayer—that your individual soul or breath is singing and dancing with the Soul of the Universe by the things you say or do today. It certainly has the potential for lifting us up out of our worries and connecting us with an abundant flow of energy.

There are a wide range of melodies that various talented people have created in recent years for singing "Kol ha-neshahmah t'hah-leil Yah" with joy and intensity. You can find lots of options on You Tube or from your favorite cantor, rabbi, or prayer leader. But most of all, remember to breathe when you sing or say this final phrase from Psalm 150, because in fact you are one of the breathing, re-markable souls that is partnering with the Source of Life with every breath and action that you take.

- Option C for Connecting with Words of Love. As a more personalized and spontaneous version, you can sit down and write your own genuine love note or words of connection to the One who possibly breathed life into you, who might be there to give you strength and energy when you need it the most, and who guides us on how to be a loving partner in taking good care of nature, our loved ones, and all the other creations that are vulnerable and fragile. What are the words from your own heart that you would like to say in writing, or silently in your head, or out loud in a spontaneous conversa-tion, to the Creative Source of all that you have been given?

Please know that I'm not saying you must do this, or that you should do this. Some people are simply not comfortable writing, saying or singing tender words of love, and they especially don't want to be pushed to say it in a false or insincere way. I appreciate what-ever is your truth about any hesitations you have about composing or saying a "love note." I'm simply offering a few options you can consider when you feel ready for writing, or for saying silently or out loud, an honest "love note" as a way of experiencing the two-way mutual relationship that each of us can have with the awesome Presence that is pulsing and energizing this world constantly.

Here, to end this chapter about love, are two quick examples of diverse types of Jews who wrote or spoke a "love note" of appre-ciation and awe for the first time in their lives (and they began to understand what it means to be in a loving partnership with the One who is beyond description). See if any of these examples sound like you or someone you know:

- Julia is a counseling client doing extremely well in her ca-reer, but she has some intensely harsh and critical thoughts that run through her head each day. Raised by two parents who are perfectionistic, hard-working, and unrelenting, Julia often feels that her busy life and her many achievements are "never quite enough."

Julia had recently ended a relationship with someone who, like Julia's parents, had been very intense and judgmental. When Julia first called my voice-mail in order to set up a counseling appoint-ment, she mentioned the fact that the referral had come from her best friend since college, who is a dynamic woman who had recently gotten trained to become a Jewish pastoral counselor for helping people discover a soothing, spiritual approach to dealing with their illnesses and challenges. Julia commented during that first phone call and during her initial counseling session, "I wish I could replace the harsh, judgmental noise inside my head with something far more compassionate, supportive, and uplifting like what my longtime friend seems to be able to do."

So in my counseling office, we experimented with several different ways to soften the internal noise from her always-churning, never-quite-satisfied brain. I wasn't sure whether or not to mention any specifically Jewish methods for Julia because I wanted to respect her particular way of discussing or exploring spiritual topics.

When I asked Julia what she was comfortable or uncomfortable with regarding spiritual or religious issues, Julia told me that she had been a twice-a-year-goes-to-services Jew ever since age 13 and had felt spiritual sometimes when she was in a yoga class or out walking in nature. But she had never felt much of a connection to the harsh, judgmental sense of God that her parents had given her as a young child.

So I asked Julia if anyone had ever mentioned the word "Shekhinah" to her (which some people describe as the feminine aspect of the Divine, while others describe the Shekhinah as a non-gendered Presence or life force that dwells within us and around us when we open up to that comforting infusion of positive energy).

Julia was quite surprised (and had never known previously) that in Judaism there has always been a word for the compassionate, in-dwelling Presence and that when we breathe calmly, or walk mindfully, or open up in song and prayer, we are connecting with the supportive energies of the Shekhinah, the flow of strength and guidance that isn't far away but rather is in our hearts and our breathing.

After that conversation in my counseling office, Julia began to read some books and articles about the Jewish sense of Shekhinah, the in-dwelling Presence, and she experimented for several weeks setting aside just ten minutes a week to write a "love letter" to that comforting Presence. Here is one of the brief "love notes" she wrote in the middle of a busy day to a wise, supportive Presence:

"My mind started racing just now and I was feeling fragmented and overloaded. But when I breathe in and out calmly, I can feel You breathing within me and all around me. You are like the gentle wind that makes the trees dance and makes me feel refreshed. You are like the bursts of intuition and innovation that come to me when I am quiet enough to listen to You. I am so sorry for all the times when I put up distance or shut You out. You are so patient and loving for the fact that you come back to me each time I invite You warmly and breathe with You once again."

Most of us aren't as poetic and articulate as Julia. But in your own authentic and plenty-good-enough words, what would you like to say to the soothing wind, the bright sunlight, the subtle intuitions, and the warm support that you sometimes sense is there for you when you open up and let it in. What kind of "love note" would you like to write to the in-dwelling Presence?

- Jonathan is someone who was raised in a very observant family and he knows how to recite the traditional prayers easily and rapidly. For many years he has taken his prayer book with him whenever he travels on business or on vacation. But he admitted to me (when we talked in private after one of my workshops) that he often looks at his watch and feels as if he is in a constant race to finish the daily prayers quicker today than he did the day before.

As Jonathan described, "I'm sure that once upon a time, David or Solomon or Moses spontaneously spoke these psalms and traditional prayers with complete honesty and passion. But for me, they are like a daily responsibility that I perform dutifully but they don't mean very much to me personally. I guess that's what can happen after thousands of years being removed from the original spark that motivated these holy words."

During our one-on-one conversation off to the side of the podium at the workshop where we met, I wasn't sure what to say to Jonathan. I sensed that Jonathan was still very committed to the importance of reciting the traditional prayers daily, but that he was also looking for the possibility of a deeper, more personal connection. Yet I wasn't exactly sure, and I didn't want to assume anything or disrespect his wishes.

So I asked Jonathan, "Can you tell me what you would like from our conversation right now?"

Jonathan thought for a moment and replied, "I guess I'm wondering if it's enough that I just say the prayers quickly each day. Does there really have to be some deep, profound, touchy-feely connection in addition to just saying the words."

He smiled and I smiled back. I loved that he was being honest about his concern of not wanting to become "too touchy-feely."

I replied, "I'm okay with whatever you choose. But I'm curious about whether you want me to noodge you a little to make the words more personal and possibly open you up to a deeper, here-and-now connection to HaShem?"

Jonathan was silent for a moment. Then a sad look came to his eyes and he said to me, "I guess that closeness is what I'm wishing I had. I know how to say endless formulaic words of praise to HaShem. But do I also sense a loving connection or a warm embrace? Not really. I'd be lying if I said I'm lovey-dovey in those moments."

Then he paused and asked with genuine curiosity, "Do you think that after all these years of going through the motions and being dutiful, I could possibly make the shift to saying these words with a true feeling of love and warmth?"

That was the beginning of Jonathan trying out an experiment. For the next several weeks, we corresponded by email and he kept me up to date on how he was doing in his quest for a more loving and intimate relationship with the Eternal One that he had been praying to so dutifully for many years in a rushed, impersonal way.

Seven weeks after we first met, I received an email from Jonathan in which he enclosed a quite vulnerable "love letter" he had written to God. Some of the words Jonathan wrote were:

"I don't like to use the word 'love' unless I really mean it. I've never felt comfortable being pressured to placate a girlfriend or any of my family members with an insincere 'I love you' or responding to someone's 'I love you' by saying a less-than-honest 'Love you too.' It always felt forced and fake. But I'm starting to realize that You, HaShem, have been my daily companion for many years and I never really took a moment to look into my heart and say how much You mean to me and how much I look to You for guidance on how to walk in Your ways. This isn't easy for me to say, but I want You to know that I am slowly discovering it's possible to love You with all my heart, with all my soul, and with all my being—and not just to recite those words quickly in order to finish the daily prayers in record time. This time I really mean it when I say the ancient phrase, 'And these words shall be upon my heart.'"

If you are also someone who is careful about not tossing around the word "love" in a manipulative or insincere way, please continue to honor that sense of integrity. Then when you sit down for just a few minutes and write a personal note to the Infinite Source of Blessings, see whether or not you feel comfortable using the word "love" and if it feels genuine to you. I've found with many counseling clients and friends that these love notes shouldn't be forced or obligatory. You might even write a love note that expresses your hesitations, such as,

"I wish I could feel complete love right now, but in fact I'm still a little bit held back because of a particular unresolved issue."

By telling your genuine truth to the One who is always open to your truth, you will be able to peel off one more layer of distance between you and the ever-flowing Source of Life. You will possibly be able to experience a little more love and open up clearer levels of connection and partnership.

CHAPTER FOUR:

Starting a Conversation About Important Topics

Consider this for a moment:

What if you looked at your cell phone right now and you saw a text message that said, "You are invited to converse personally with the mysterious Source of the Universe and please bring a list of topics that are important to you."

Would you:

a) Roll your eyes and delete the text message because you suspect it's a prank.

Or b) Show the text message to someone you trust and ask, "Is this for real? Can you look it up on Google or Snopes to see if it's been debunked already?"

Or c) Let go of the need to prove how the text message originated, and instead use this moment as a welcome, spontaneous opportunity to ask, "What are the important topics you would want to discuss if you could very soon have an intimate conversation with the Creative Source, the Breath of Life?"

The reason I'm asking you this question about "Inviting You Personally to Converse About Important Topics" is because that is exactly what happens at nearly every Jewish prayer service (or in your own personal prayers at home or in nature) when you get to a specific section called "The Amidah" (the Standing Prayer), which also is sometimes called "The Tefilah," (the Major Prayer), or also called "the Sh'mohneh Esreih," (the 18 Blessings—and a 19th blessing was added 2,100 years ago during the Roman period).

In this ancient but very here-and-now-in-this-current-moment prayer, you are being given a genuine invitation to tap into your heart, your emotions, your longings for your future, and your recent frustrations—and then to pour out those feelings and desires in a whispered conversation with the Source of Life.

This may sound like a complete surprise to you about what happens all over the world during the Standing Prayer during every weekday, holiday, or holiday service, especially if you grew up in a congregation where you were told to just be quiet and listen politely to the people leading the service, or if you were taught to race through the prayers quickly.

You might be asking, "Is the Amidah, the Standing Prayer, really about having an intimate, authentic conversation with the pulsing Source of Life?" Or you might be wondering, "What if I am unsure about believing in God? What if I am just standing up, opening my heart, and sharing my concerns, but I'm still not certain about believing?"

The way I see it as a psychologist is that we humans have two choices: We can keep our deepest feelings and concerns locked inside. Or we can find a safe place to tell the truth and explore what's truly important to us—and to stop hiding from what's churning inside us. The Jewish tradition is to set aside a few moments for a "Standing Prayer," in which you rise up and (for a minute or several minutes) you are invited to speak your deepest feelings in a hushed whisper that no one around you can hear (but that you and the mysterious Flow of Creation and Compassion can experience).

Many Jews today have never had this moment of honesty and release explained to them. Yet if you take a quick look on the internet, you will find on the Chabad site that it says, "The Amidah (the Standing Prayer) is the centerpiece of the prayer service, wherein we beseech God for all our personal and communal needs." Many Conservative Jewish rabbis describe the Amidah as "addressing the Infinite One from the depths of your soul." In addition, many Reform and Reconstructionist Jewish rabbis describe the personal requests and conversations in the Amidah section of the prayer book (conversing with God, or the Shekhinah—the in-dwelling Presence, or the still small voice within us) as "the central prayer of the service."

Just like Hannah, a Jewish woman in the Biblical "First Book of Samuel" (who was upset and worried about being childless and so she poured out her feelings in a hushed whisper that no one could hear but they could see her lips were moving), we Jews are definitely invited during the Standing Prayer to speak our most important concerns and longings in a hushed voice with our lips moving and our hearts open. For more than 2,000 years, Jews from every part of the world have stood up from their seats for several minutes during the Amidah prayer and in an intimate whisper said essentially, "This is what I'm passionately hoping for. This is what I'm needing help to make happen. This is what I'm concerned about and I don't want to hide from these feelings or be silent any longer."

In this chapter, I will be exploring with you several different ways that Jews in the 21st century get "up close and personal" with their innermost feelings during the Standing Prayer. Whether you are very traditional, a little bit traditional, very untraditional, or brand new to the entire idea of having a whispered personal conversation about important topics, I am hoping these various, permitted methods for making this prayer come alive for you and your loved ones will help you raise up your energy and your clarity for moving forward in your life.

The various Jewish methods for saying and experiencing the deeper meanings of the Amidah prayer (the Standing Prayer) include:

- Option #1: Understanding in a deeper way what the ancient rabbis were passionate about and how some of these concerns still resonate for you or me today.

- Option #2: Using your own words, insights, and experiences to re-interpret the specific topics that are found in the Amidah section of the prayer book.

- Option #3: Making sure that for at least a few moments, and possibly for much of the Amidah prayer, you are speaking your truth and opening up your heart to your deeply felt concerns.

I promise you that you don't need to settle for just one of the above three options (the rabbinic words, the current re-interpretations, or the personal, spontaneous words). Many people today when they are at a congregational prayer service, or when they pray at home or in nature, choose a hybrid combination that includes some of the traditional blessings that have been in the prayer books for thousands of years, some modern interpretations of the ancient topics, and definitely some spontaneous words from your own heart (especially during the section of the Amidah prayer where it specifically asks for your own words of prayer, meditation, or silent contemplation).

To be completely honest, there is one thing I need to say upfront about this Jewish tradition of asking, beseeching, or opening up your heart and pouring out your concerns. Please note that there is no guarantee that your topics will get solved exactly on the spot. Most Jewish scholars are in agreement that God is not the same as an

ATM machine where you put in a plastic card and easily withdraw exactly the amount of cash you desire in less than a minute.

Rather, there is a beautiful moment in Jewish spirituality, especially in the Standing Prayer where your heart is open, your soul is significantly elevated, and you can be fully honest and real in front of the One who breathed you into this world and who continues to connect your individual pulse to the ongoing pulse and energy of the moon, the tides, the winds, the nutrients of the Earth, and all the various intuitions and good ideas that can sometimes help you make progress on an important longing.

From a completely different perspective, imagine for a moment that you are a trained anthropologist, or an investigative journalist, or a documentary filmmaker from the planet Saturn coming here to Earth to do a research study about Jewish individuals in the 21st century. If you were from another planet and you closely watched sincere Jews doing the passionate requests of the Standing Prayer for several minutes, you would be taking notes about the fact that these Jews seem to be whispering with intensity (to an unseen Presence or Life Force) and you might say, "Wow! These Jewish individuals are able to connect deeply with unseen levels of existence. They're not shy about being honest and real. They are so alive, expressive, and energized in ways that we don't experience here on boring and overly-cautious Saturn."

Now, here back on Earth, I want to offer you some important details for the three different options of how to make the Standing Prayer more engaging and more meaningful for you and your loved ones:

Option #1: Utilizing Some of the Beautiful Aspects of the Traditional, By-the-Book "Standing Prayer" Words and Phrases

In its original form written many centuries ago, the Standing Prayer has some fascinating gems and uplifting moments that many people race through quickly, but if you understand these phrases on a deeper level and take them to heart, they can become far more meaningful and inspiring for you or your loved ones. For instance:

A First Gem to Consider: The Opening Words and Physical Movements that Get Your Body and Mind Ready for a Deep Conversation

In every prayer book for congregations, or when you pray at home or in nature, there is an opening phrase immediately at the start of the Standing Prayer. You might have seen several people take three small steps backward and then three small steps forward when they say or sing this opening phrase. It's as though you are telling your body and your mind, "Step back three small steps for a moment in order to be humble and in awe of the amazing Presence or Energy you are going to converse with. Then from a place of humility and awe, feel free to step forward three small steps and experience that you are in a genuine, legitimate conversation of soul to Soul and that you are going to be fully present and able to connect with this awesome Breath of Life."

The exact words of the opening phrase are: "Adonai, s'fah-tahy teef-takh oo-fee yah-ghid t'hee-lah-tekha, Eternal One, open my lips that my mouth may declare Your gloriousness."

In other words, "Please help me at this exact moment to be conscious that this is not just some mundane conversation about trivial matters. Please help my thoughts and my words for the next few minutes to rise up to a genuine conversation that is true and meaningful between my soul and Your Soul."

I love the fact that in Judaism there is often this simultaneous combination of humility and dignity. We take three small steps backward to appreciate we are just human and then we immediately take three small steps forward to appreciate that we are able to rise up and have an honest conversation with the incredible Source of Life.

There is a wonderful teaching from Rabbi Simcha Bunim Bonhardt, a Hasidic master from 300 years ago, who suggested that we Jews should have two reminder notes in our two pockets as we travel through life. In one pocket the note essentially says, "I am just one person among millions of people, like a tiny grain of sand in the desert." In the other pocket the note essentially says, "The entire world was created so that you and I could be alive at this moment having meaning, purpose and connection to an elevated path." Humility and dignity—in combination at each moment.

So when you take three small steps backward in humility and then three small steps forward in dignity so that you can converse with the Infinite Source, please notice if your body and mind are starting to enter the Standing Prayer with a sense of awe, appreciation, and warm connection. This quick moment (of going back a little and then forward a little) is also reminding us that even when we take a small temporary step backward on our personal journeys of becoming our full creative, compassionate selves, we can still be resilient and go three steps forward to get closer to the fully-actualized person we were created to be.

You might also have noticed during the Standing Prayer that some people bow or bend from the hips each time they say the words "Barukh Atah (Blessed are You)" out of respect and humility. But then they immediately raise up again to a full standing position at the word "Adonai (Eternal One)" in order to speak directly to the Divine Presence (not out of ego but rather as a sense that we are invited to have an intimate, one-on-One, soul-to-Soul conversation from an upright, dignified posture).

The next time you say or sing the Standing Prayer, see what it feels like to you to take three small steps backward and three small steps forward at the start of the prayer, as well as bowing for the words "Barukh Atah Blessed are You" and rising back up to a full standing position at the word "Adonai Eternal One." Does it feel as if you can be simultaneously humble and profoundly intimate with the Source of Life at the same time? Does it stir up a feeling of awe and genuine connection to this moment in which you are going to have an honest conversation with whatever you personally believe to be the pulsing Source of the universe?

A Second Gem to Consider: That You Are Part of a Long Legacy of People Who Have Also Had These Intimate Conversations

The next paragraph of the Standing Prayer describes the ancestors and the many generations that came before us and who also had deep longings and deep connecting moments with the Source of Life. The words in the prayer book say, "Blessed is the One Who remembers the kindnesses of the ancestors and Who redeems their children's children with love."

In other words, when you stand in the Presence of the Creative Source having a sincere conversation with the Breath of Life, you are not alone. You bring with you all the good deeds and all the conversations of your lineage going all the way back to Abraham, Sarah, Isaac, Rebecca, Jacob, Rachel, and Leah, as well as any of your parents, grandparents, great-grandparents or other mentors and supportive souls whose shoulders you are standing on today in order to rise up and become your fullest self.

Sometimes when I am in a synagogue, or in nature, or at home, and I say these words about the kindnesses of our ancestors and the connection that transmits love and guidance from generation to generation, I sense a tiny glimmer of some of their insights, their tenderness, and their souls being present as I converse with the One that is hard to describe. I feel at those moments that we are entering a timeless possibility where we are all gathered together as one and we are engaged in a conversation and a creative process of repairing the world that has the momentum and energy of many, many generations.

One time when I was saying and singing the words of the Standing Prayer, my mind flashed back to Alex Haley, the very dignified and courageous man who researched his ancestral roots in Africa and wrote the bestseller "Roots" that caused millions of people from all races and ethnicities to start looking for their own roots and influences. I met Alex Haley several times when I worked at Doubleday Publishing in New York during my 20's and I remember him saying that sometimes at night in his dreams and sometimes during waking moments on difficult days when he closes his eyes and thinks of his ancestors, he experiences a feeling of their presence, their strength, their courage, and their resilience carrying him forward with whatever is challenging him at the current moment.

So when you or I say in the Standing Prayer, "Who remembers the kindnesses of my ancestors and Who redeems their children's children with love," I'm wondering if we can actually feel the love, the courage, and the strength that our ancestors had (and that we can be uplifted by) as we say or sing the words of the ancestor paragraph of the Standing Prayer.

Instead of just mouthing the words with little or no emotion, what if you brought to mind:

- Who are the people from your own lineage who had the courage to stand up for important causes or for treating people with dignity and kindness, even when others weren't doing so?

- Who are the people that you met when you were young, or whose stories inspired you (even though you never met the actual individual), that you can bring to mind as you converse during the Standing Prayer with the Source of Life who "remembers the kindnesses of our ancestors."

- Who are the role models in your life that have inspired you to learn more, love more, care more, and listen more?

You might feel like a grain of sand sometimes, but you also bring a rich history with you when you stand in the presence of the Eternal One. Even if your ancestors or role models didn't have much money or easy lives, their courage and their insights are still a part of who you are today. The Standing Prayer starts by appreciating these inspirations from your past.

A Third Gem to Consider: The Mystical Words "Kadosh, Kadosh, Kadosh" and the Desire to Raise Yourself Up to Be One of the Angels of Repair and Goodness in This World

A few paragraphs into the Standing Prayer, there is a fascinating moment when people say the words "holy, holy, holy, kadosh, kadosh, kadosh" and you see many people going up onto their tiptoes three times quickly as they say those words. What the heck is going on?

The profound verse "kadosh, kadosh, kadosh" comes from a vision by the prophet Isaiah in which he saw celestial beings (possibly angels or energies that were not tied down by earthly limitations) who were doing the holy work of creation and doing it joyfully. In Judaism, we don't tend to envision angels as chubby round cherubs like you see in a lot of medieval art. Rather, we tend to think of angels (and humans who are doing compassionate, creative, reparative holy work) as spiritual and moral entities who are rising above the physical limits and sluggishness of having a human body.

So when you rise up on your tiptoes three times as you say "kadosh, kadosh, kadosh" during the Standing Prayer, you can imagine yourself rising up from the physical limits of your body or your situation, and becoming even more of the spiritual, moral, creative self you are capable of being. You can envision yourself becoming more like an angel (or a vehicle for transmitting spiritual energy and compassionate help) as you partner with the Creative Source to make this world an even more beautiful and compassionate place. You don't have to do it alone, but if you find your own individual way to raise up your energy sometimes to an angelic level and you partner with other souls who also are willing to raise up their energies to an angelic level, a lot of good things can happen.

As you go up on your tiptoes and say "kadosh, kadosh, kadosh" the next time you sing or say the Standing Prayer, please bring to mind what are the actions in your life that you can say to the Source of Creation are your ways of being one of God's angels? What are the creative or compassionate things you would like to do more of in the future? In your conversation with the Source of Life, can you feel a sense of partnership that you are one of the earthly-yet-spiritual beings who are part of the ongoing repair of this world?

Then notice that with each rise onto your tiptoes during "kadosh, kadosh, kadosh," you not only go up, but you also return to a solid, grounded footing all three times. We are not only rising up to the heights in this prayer, but we are also returning each time to our connection to life on Earth and taking firm steps forward in a grounded, centered way.

A Fourth Gem to Consider: Asking for the Eternal One to Bless Israel

For thousands of years during the Standing Prayer, Jews have asked the Creative Source to protect Jerusalem, the city of wholeness and peace (Yeru means city and Shalayim means wholeness and peace), to gather us from the four corners of the Earth to once again rebuild Jerusalem, and to spread the teachings of how to treat one another with kindness from a renewed Jerusalem.

In other words, the Standing Prayer has always been a chance to ask for peace, to ask for guidance on how to achieve peace, and to raise up our energy and our own actions to pursue peace.

These requests for peace in Jerusalem are found both in the middle paragraphs of the Standing Prayer and also in one of the final paragraphs of the Standing Prayer, a paragraph called either "Sim Shalom – Grant Us Peace" or "Shalom Rav — the Abundant Peace or the Great Peace."

As you say or sing the visionary requests for peace spreading from Jerusalem, it can bring up all sorts of feelings and concerns. What do you personally think is the next step toward peace? What kinds of insights, new approaches, new possibilities and shared strength do you want to experience right now as you say the ancient phrases about Jerusalem in the Standing Prayer? What kinds of partnerships and teamwork will be needed in order to move closer toward peace in your lifetime or in our children's lifetime? This is one of the important conversations we are invited to have when we engage in the Standing Prayer.

A Fifth Gem to Consider: What Are We Going to Teach and Model for Future Generations?

There is a fascinating line in the middle of the Standing Prayer that says, "L'dor va-dor nah-ghid gahd-lekha," which means, "We will declare Your greatness through all the generations."

In some congregations they repeat or sing the words several times. At the congregation where I attend services, we put our arms around one another as we sing one of several beautiful melodies that have been written for "L'dor va-dor, from generation to generation."

As you sing or say, "L'dor va-dor, from generation to generation," please feel free to envision yourself interacting with your kids, or your grandkids, or your niece or nephew, or your students, or a younger sibling or cousin in your family, or any young person you have the joy of interacting with in your current life or in the next several decades. What are the ways that you want to inspire or model for this young individual what it means to be a good person? What are the ways that you want to demonstrate for this young person what it means to be a healthy, curious, compassionate, and alive Jewish soul in the 21st century? What are the ways you want to do a better job teaching Jewish wisdom and Jewish joy to the next generation than it was taught to you?

In essence, as you converse with the Eternal One during the Standing Prayer, you are saying, "I am Your partner in this ongoing, important project of creating, repairing, and raising up the level of compassion in this fragile world. I truly appreciate how much I have been given and I promise to share these gifts with people in a loving way...L'dor va-dor, from generation to generation."

A Sixth Gem to Consider: The Absolute Permission to Share Your Personal Concerns Without Embarrassment or Loss of Privacy

Now we get to one of the most amazing parts of the Standing Prayer. For thousands of years, Jews have set aside a few minutes just to say it like it is. It even says in the Talmud that every time we say the Standing Prayer there must be at least one personal prayer that comes from your own heart. You can ask for anything, you can complain about anything, you can strategize about anything, you can be sad or angry or hopeful or inspired about anything. This is your moment to converse in a hushed whisper to the Creative Flow of the Universe who is possibly right there in front of you and within your heart.

What would you like to talk about today? Or do you prefer to just be silent and listen to see what emerges? Or do you choose to just breathe and connect in a sense of gratitude or oneness?

Or do you have some stored up concerns or feelings that you finally are ready to pour out today?

It's your choice and at the end of the "Silent Prayer" section of the Standing Prayer there is a lovely phrase that people sing or recite, which says, "May the expressions of my mouth and the thoughts of my heart be accepted by You…" It is an intimate moment of saying, "I deeply want to connect with You, and I want You to have the truth that I don't usually share with just anyone." It is a moment of holy relationship.

Now that we've explored a few (and definitely not all) of the deeper meanings of what you will find in most prayer books for the 18 or 19 blessings of the Standing Prayer, we are ready to consider a slightly different way of doing this daily or weekly prayer. Please take a breath for a moment because for some people this will seem controversial and a little unusual. But for many centuries and with the support of many rabbis and teachers, there is a tradition of sometimes questioning, disagreeing, re-interpreting, or fine-tuning some of the ancient phrases of the Standing Prayer. Here's Option #2, a respectful way to practice the Jewish tradition of "Yisra-Eil, wrestling with the Eternal One" as part of the Standing Prayer.

Option #2: Using Your Own Words, Insights, and Experiences to Re-Interpret Some of the Phrases of the Standing Prayer.

There are a few of the 18 or 19 blessings in the Standing Prayer that were quite passionate and important to the ancient rabbis who compiled the prayer. But they are a bit controversial or confusing for us moderns.

For instance, there is a line that says, "Restore the judges as in days of old." If you look at that phrase and it sounds to you like the ancient rabbis are asking for there to be a theocracy once again in which a member of the Levite lineage gets to be the High Priest, while a Sanhedrin (a religious court) gets to make all the final decisions about everyone who lives in Israel (and all Jews worldwide), your intestines might clutch a bit and your brain might start racing with all sorts of ways that you and specific people you care about would not do well in a nation run by a strictly religious legal authority.

But rather than freaking out and saying, "That's the last straw—I'm outta here. I don't want to pray or be Jewish if it means there's gonna be a High Priest running the show," how about if we take a breath and do what Jews have done for thousands of years: Let's have a discussion about something important, and do it lovingly and reasonably to see what it really means to "Restore the judges as in days of old."

If you want to be the first one to speak, please go ahead. What is your personal interpretation of the phrase "Restore the judges as in days of old?" When you think of judges, courts, law enforcement personnel, and the legal system, what would you like to pray and ask for if you were in a one-on-One conversation with the Source of Compassion and Justice? What would you like to say to the Creator of the Universe about what kind of legal system you would like to see created now and in the future?

Or if you want to chill for a few seconds and listen to a few other opinions about what the phrase "Restore the judges as in days of old" might mean on deeper levels, here are a few quick possibilities:

- There's a book called "The Amidah: Traditional Prayers, Modern Commentaries" by Rabbi Lawrence Hoffman in which he quotes from several prominent rabbis and scholars (who come from each of the branches of Judaism) on how they deal with several controversial lines like this one about "restoring the judges as in days of old" from the Standing Prayer.

One of the prominent teachers that Hoffman quotes is Rabbi David Ellenson, who grew up in an Orthodox family, trained to become a Reform Rabbi, has taught at the rabbinic schools for several branches of Judaism in the United States and in Israel, and has been a leader for many years at the rabbinic school of Hebrew Union College. Rabbi Ellenson writes, "Several aspects of this phrase about restoring the judges have proved troublesome to moderns."

He then goes on to explain that in the 1975 prayer book "Gates of Prayer" and in the 1995 and 2007 revised prayer books that were developed more recently, the rabbinic teams that compiled the prayers chose to focus not on re-establishing the High Priests of ancient days, but rather to focus on the kind of fair, impartial, and compassionate judicial system we all long for, would like to pray for, and that the Torah described (way ahead of its time) in Leviticus as "You shall not render an unjust judgment; you shall not be partial to the poor or defer to the great or wealthy: with justice you shall judge your neighbor."

I hope you won't mind if I repeat those exquisite words from Leviticus that were spoken and written many centuries ahead of the rest of the world: "you shall not be partial to the poor or defer to the great or wealthy...with justice you shall judge your neighbor."

At a time in history when bribes, status, and threats of violence were commonplace in courts and law enforcement, the Torah had a very different approach and said clearly, "Don't let someone's outward appearance, status, income, or reputation determine whether they are guilty or innocent of a crime. Make sure you are assessing what actually happened based on an unbiased view that creates a fair and peaceful society."

This was a radical viewpoint several thousand years ago when it first emerged in the Torah and it's still something we aspire to achieve more consistently today (in a world where there are still judgments being made and people being treated unfairly based on outward appearance, social status, income, or favors being given to those in power).

In other words, the Standing Prayer phrase "Restore the judges as in days of old" now gets interpreted by the vast majority of people who say it in a one-on-One conversation with the Source of Life as "Please guide us on how to make judges, courts, police forces, and legal systems more reliably fair and unbiased—like it says in the Torah."

Another voice in this discussion about "what are we praying for when we pray and work for justice in our society and throughout the world" comes from Rabbi Zalman Schachter-Shalomi, who grew up Orthodox in Europe, became a beloved campus rabbi for thousands of teens and young adults for many years in the United States and Canada, and then was the founder of the progressive Jewish Renewal movement that attempts to bring more aliveness, Jewish joy and respect for diversity to each of the branches of Judaism.

In his 2005 book "Jewish with Feeling," Reb Zalman talks about the Standing Prayer and the section about "restoring the judges as in days of old" in his very personalized, from-the-heart tone of voice as he writes, "Finally, we are at the highest point in the davvening (a Yiddish word for passionate prayer) as we reach the silent Amidah (the Standing Prayer). I find when I stand in silence at that highest place…that all my concerns start coming to the surface. I always encourage people who are saying the Amidah to express their own thoughts in any of the nineteen blessings. So when I talk with HaShem about restoring our judges as of old, I sometimes say, 'Oy God, I'm worried about the state of justice in our country. We are not treating rich and poor alike with justice, as Torah told us to do. Please guide our leaders and appoint fair judges. Please help all of us to judge our fellow beings with compassion."

Notice the warm, conversational tone of voice that Reb Zalman brings to the conversations with the Eternal Source. Is that one-on-One intimacy and warmth something you have done in the past or might be willing to experiment with in the future: to talk with God in such a spontaneous, honest, partnership kind of way and to say, "Oy God, I'm worried about this" or to ask, "Creative Source that Flows Continually, I need your help here to come up with ideas and persistence on how to reduce the suffering I see every day lately that is so unfair."

As one more perspective on the Amidah phrase, "restore the judges as in days of old," there have also been a number of discussions in the various Orthodox communities in Israel, the United States, and throughout the world about "do we really want to pray for a return to a theocratic High Priest ruling over Israel and all of world Jewry, or do we want to interpret 'restore the judges as in days of old' in a different way than that." In the highly-respected Orthodox prayer book "The Complete Artscroll Siddur," there is a footnote on page 106 that says under the phrase "restore our judges as in earliest times" the following words: "A secondary theme of this prayer is the wish that God help all judges rule wisely and justly."

Now let's see what might happen if we truly prayed with our hearts and with our actions about "restoring our judges to the fairness and unbiased level that was first described in the ancient words of the Torah." Consider for a moment: When have you seen judges, attorneys, police officers, eyewitnesses, or people at a dinner party do or say things that were unfair, biased, or unjust? Are you willing to pray for guidance and to align with those who care deeply about fixing what's broken in the legal system (and in our polarized society) for establishing fairness now and in the future?

One of the things I love about Judaism (and you can see it in these modern interpretations of the Standing Prayer words about "restoring the judges as in days of old") is that when you or I stand up during a moment of prayer and have a conversation with the Source of Life about "what are we gonna do to make our legal system and our society more fair and just," I love the fact that we are not just asking for God's insights, energy, and intervention to improve things, but we are also waking ourselves up to the fact that we need to do our part of the human-Divine partnership—we need to pay attention to what's broken and to work to make things more just and unbiased.

This prayer phrase about judges and justice truly comes alive if we say it sincerely in our current decade. Nearly every human being with a functioning heart who watched the video of George Floyd being murdered in 2020 in broad daylight in front of a convenience store in Minneapolis knows that there is work to do and that it's going to take a lot of wisdom, persistence, and creativity to bring fairness to our world and to overcome our subconscious biases.

The next time you are saying the Standing Prayer in a congregation, or at home, or in nature, please tap into your own heart during the line "restore the judges as in days of old" and see what comes up as to what you personally believe that the Source of Life can do to improve things and what we humans can do to improve things. Is there some under-represented individual or group you want to learn more about, so that you can align with organizations that work to get the kind of fairness and respect these under-represented individuals deserve? Is there some flaw in the human-designed system of justice-seeking that you (or an organization that you support) can fix or improve before more lives are harmed by prejudiced thinking? That's what Rabbi Abraham Joshua Heschel (who marched with Martin Luther King, Jr in Selma) would describe as "praying with your feet," which means to not only speak the words of longing but also to turn your heartfelt prayer words into good ideas for action steps and teamwork that can improve things now and in the future.

A Quick Look at One More Controversy in the Standing Prayer

There is one more line in the first sections of the Standing Prayer that most people race through as "No big deal," but in fact it is a very important topic that in today's world is quite controversial and crucial to our survival.

It says in the Standing Prayer that we are to recite for half the year (the late Spring and Summer months), "You cause the dew to fall" and for the other half of the year (the Fall and Winter months), "You cause the wind to blow and the rain to fall."

If you have ever said the Standing Prayer in a congregation that goes quickly through the lines of the prayer, you might have had little or no emotion or personal connection to those words as you recited them dutifully.

But if you stop and think about it for a moment, we are back to the important issue of, "What exactly is the partnership between the Source of Life and we human beings who are the earthly stewards that have the shared responsibility of taking care of God's creations one day at a time—locally and globally."

If you live in a drought-prone part of the world that has insufficient rain and shortages of good drinking water, the prayer that says, "You cause the dew to fall" is about life-or-death because daily amounts of morning dew are what we need to prevent droughts, fires, and devastation. We can be grateful to the Creator that even in a desert climate there is a reliable morning dew (I hope it remains reliable!!) which keeps the vegetation alive and reduces the fire danger. But we can't just rely on the Creator for this morning dew, because we now know that with climate change and global warming there are more fires, more droughts, more water shortages, and less morning dew. We humans need to enter into that Standing Prayer conversation with the Creator and say not only, "Thank you for the morning dew during the summer months," but also, "I am your partner in caring for this delicate ecosystem you have given us. I need to do my part to reverse global warming. Here's what I am able to do starting right now and what I am willing to do in an ongoing way."

The same type of conversation can happen during the half a year when we say, "Thank you for making the winds blow and the rain to fall." Those are the months when we can remember during the Standing Prayer that we are partners with the Creator and we need to work on reversing the climate crisis because otherwise the winds, hurricanes, tornadoes, floods, and farm-destroying storms will cause additional deaths, food shortages and chaos.

For many years I didn't have a clue regarding what was important or energizing about the Standing Prayer phrases "Who causes the dew to fall" and "Who causes the winds to blow and the rains to fall." But ever since I began learning more about climate change and the devastation and suffering caused by it, I now say those two lines as a call-to-action that I am ready and willing to do more to reverse global warming.

What about you? If during the Standing Prayer you feel in your heart for even just a moment a sense of the partnership between the One Who Creates and we humans who are very responsible for whether that amazing creation will survive and flourish, what kinds of specific actions and steps will you take in order to heal this fragile planet we live on? Suddenly in the middle of the Standing Prayer you are not just saying empty words about "morning dew" or "winds and rain," but you are lifting up your awareness and your energy to be part of the solutions our world so desperately needs right now.

Option #3: Making Sure You Go Deeply into a Private Space During the Standing Prayer So You Can Emerge with Renewed Energy

Now I'm going to end this chapter about the Standing Prayer by focusing on a few creative ways to deepen your experience of having a private one-on-One connection with your personal sense of the Breath of Life or the Creative Source. Please continue to develop your own unique style for doing this energizing prayer, but here are a few possibilities in case you want to try something different every so often.

First of all, you may have noticed that some people in various congregations cover their heads with a tallit (a prayer shawl) and create a private sanctuary for some or all of the Standing Prayer moments with the Ever-flowing Source. What would that be like for you? If you were wrapped in a sacred garment and you had the privacy under that improvised "tent of meeting" to whisper your most honest and genuine thoughts during the Standing Prayer, would that enhance your sense of connection and closeness to the One that is beyond human descriptions? Would it help you feel free of the sounds and visual distractions for a few minutes so that you could tap into the spiritual side of who you are?

I remember the first time I saw people putting a prayer shawl over their heads during the Standing Prayer and my initial reaction was, "What? No way. That looks strange. I don't think I'm ready to do that in public."

But then a few years later, I got up the courage and I tried it out. What a surprising and beautiful ritual it has become. There is something so unusual and so comforting about being wrapped in a sacred shawl and being able to go deep into a private conversation that no other human can hear. It feels so liberating to spend a few minutes in a different reality than the agitated, distracting world we live in much of the time.

Now what would you like to say or do while you are in this private, intimate space (either under a prayer shawl or not)? Here are a few quick possibilities from a diverse group of Jews:

- **Taking a Few Minutes to Dwell on an Intriguing Word or Phrase.** Some people use the several minutes of the Silent Prayer or the Standing Prayer to focus on one word or one phrase from the prayer book that calls out to you on a particular day. For example, one of my friends told me that she recently spent the entire ten or fifteen minutes of the Standing Prayer exploring her complicated feelings about one specific Hebrew word, "Yirah," which is one of those fascinating Hebrew words that has two different meanings. "Yirah" can mean "fear" or it can also mean "awe." Or "Yirah" can be a mixture of fear and awe at the same time.

This friend of mine told me, "I saw the word 'Yirah' in the prayer book and I decided to have a real conversation with myself and with God or the In-Dwelling Presence, the Shekhinah, about how much I have lived in fear sometimes and how much I have experienced awe and amazement sometimes. I realized during this conversation that I definitely need a little bit of fear to motivate me sometimes to take action to fix things that aren't working well and to stay humble and human. Yet what I also want to connect with each day, each week, and each year is that I definitely need a lot of moments of awe and amazement in my life. I don't want to get bogged down in fear or trying to please everyone. I want to make sure that I'm staying open each day to notice all the things in nature, in the warmth of someone's touch, in the caring conversations I have with people, and in the beauty of art and creativity so that I will have a lot more awe and a lot less fear running through my veins and my nerve endings. I feel like those fifteen minutes during the Standing Prayer, when I meditated with complete honesty on the word 'Yirah, fear and awe,' were some of the most profound minutes I've ever had during a prayer service."

- **For Letting Go of Stress and Re-charging Your Batteries.** Some people use the several minutes of the Standing Prayer or the few minutes of the Silent Prayer section to focus on letting go of the worries and pressures they were feeling that day and to open up to a renewed sense of strength and creative possibilities. For example, one of my counseling clients is a man with a very stressful job who told me, "During the Standing Prayer, I usually ask for help or insights about a difficult decision or a frustrating situation I've been facing recently. I feel like those few minutes under my prayer shawl in the Standing Prayer are a safe place to let go for a moment and get quiet inside so that I can listen to an inner wisdom that comes from a mysterious place I can't quite describe. There's usually this moment under the prayer shawl where I can hear my own breathing and I can sense I am being guided by a wisdom that can see the big picture and not just the narrow power-struggles and the demanding personalities I face each day. After several minutes of letting go and listening quietly, I often feel like I've re-charged my energy and clarity for going forward in a constructive way with good momentum."

- **For Relaxing the Body and Feeling Part of a Much Greater Flow.** Some people use the Standing Prayer as a chance to move gently, breathe deeply, and unblock the energy flows in your body. For example, one of my friends from college is a woman who left Judaism for several years (and became very involved studying with some excellent teachers of Eastern religions, meditation, and yoga) partly because she had never been told that meditation, stretching/centering movements, and daily mindfulness are also key parts of Judaism. My friend eventually found some more modern Jewish teachers who helped her combine her Jewish soul with her meditation, mindfulness, and physical centering practices.

This longtime friend told me recently, "My favorite part of the Sabbath prayer service I now attend at least twice a month at a very welcoming Jewish congregation not far from where I live is when we do the Standing Prayer and I feel my body and my mind opening up with three steps backward, three steps forward, the gentle breathing, the several times of bending and then focusing upright, the three times of going up on my tiptoes, the sense of honesty and vulnerability, and the swaying to the melodies and rhythms. I feel like the physical movements and thoughtful ideas of the ten or fifteen minutes of the Standing Prayer are some of the most beautiful things I do to keep myself centered and connected to the flow of energy that I first discovered in yoga and now I find in my Jewish prayers also."

- **For Specific Requests.** Some people use the Standing Prayer as a chance to ask for very specific things and not to hold back. As one of my relatives once told me, "I figure that if God is as vast and strong as some people say, I'm probably not giving God a hernia or a headache if I ask for help or ideas for some of the complicated things that I've been dealing with lately. I figure a Life Force that is beyond gender or human limitations can handle me and my stuff a lot better than my ex-husband could."

What about you? Have you sometimes felt shy or awkward about opening up to an invisible flow of creativity, compassion and insights? Have you ever felt trapped by your own skepticism or your search for 100% certainty, so that you judged yourself as "strange" or "weak" if you started to say silently or whisper in a hushed voice, "I think I need a little bit of help or connection here. I'm tired of trying to figure it out all on my own."

If you want to get a glimpse of the bigger picture regarding something important in your life, all I can say is to invite you to experiment with this remarkable process of standing up, speaking your truth in a private, hushed voice to the One that is beyond our human limitations, and then seeing if that intimate conversation helps you to feel more open to good ideas and much-needed support. Each of us has a slightly different sense of the Creative Source that is beyond human description. Each of us has a slightly different way of conversing with that Ever-flowing Source of Insights. My hope is that you and your loved ones will find a way that works noticeably well for you on stressful weeks to renew your resilience and your creativity.

CHAPTER FIVE:

What Happens When You Pray for Healing?

A few years ago, I had to go quickly under the knife for an emergency surgery. As the nurse walked up to my gurney bed to give me a sufficient dose of the knockout fluids, I remember thinking about my young daughter who has Autism and who depends on my help a lot. I also thought about my wife who was recovering from an injured meniscus cartilage near her right knee and she sometimes needed some assistance and support.

At that vulnerable moment of entering into the hands of the nurses, the aides, the doctors, and the medicines, I began to say a prayer.

Let me stop here and ask you a personal question: What exactly would you pray for or say silently at that moment? What are the words you have been taught, or what are the spontaneous words you might say, if you were faced with that kind of urgency or uncertainty?

This chapter will explore what Jews have done in the past and especially what Jews do today when we are hoping for healing, excellent care, and good outcomes (either for yourself, or for your loved ones, or for anyone else whose health crisis touches your heart and makes you want to put out a call for help and guidance).

We will be looking at the deeper meanings and personal aspects of prayers for healing that people have said with passion and concern for many centuries. We will also be looking at different, fascinating ideas on what exactly happens when we pray for healing and support.

What Are the Settings Where You or I Might Feel the Urge to Ask for Help?

If you stop and think about it for a moment, there are all sorts of places and situations where people from many walks of life and many levels of education and income get quiet for a few seconds and say a prayer for healing. For instance:

- If you look into a waiting room at a hospital or a clinic, you might find one or several people asking silently, or in a whisper, for support and guidance because they or someone they love is facing a crucial medical test, a complicated medical procedure, or a search for answers to a lingering medical challenge.

- If you go to a Sabbath service at a temple or synagogue, you will likely see some people praying silently for healing, or you might see that this congregation has a tradition of people whispering to the rabbi or the prayer leader the name of a loved one who needs healing. Or they might have a moment during the service when people think of someone they love and hold that person in mind as they sing the beautiful Mee Sheh-bay-rakh melody of singer-songwriter Debbie Friedman, or some other version of the same prayer.

- In many families at a Friday night Shabbat candle-lighting or at various meals during the week, you will often hear someone ask for healing and support for a specific individual near or far who is going through a medical challenge. Or you might know of someone who has a list of names they pray for during their morning blessings.

Like many people, I've always been curious to learn more about what happens inside our hearts, and on unseen levels of existence, and in real-life physical and emotional terms, when these prayers are uttered with sincerity and strong intentions. How about you? Have you ever been curious what the impact might be if you or I say a passionate prayer for healing for oneself or for someone you care about a lot? Does it make some sort of difference?

What the Scientific Studies Have Said So Far

It has been estimated by several scientific researchers that more than 85% of Americans pray for healing every so often, either for themselves or for someone else. In addition, research also shows that in the United States there are more than 35,000 prayer circles (more than one person praying for healing for a few individuals that the group is focusing on). On the question of "Is it strange or is it normal to be praying for health," there seems to be a wide consensus from numerous studies that prayers for one's own health or the health of others are extremely widespread in our society, even in the 21st century.

But what about the science of whether a prayer for health makes a difference in someone's medical outcomes? For several decades, there have been dozens of studies trying to find a way to measure this mysterious aspect of life. For instance, at Duke University and several other prestigious college and research centers, there have been a series of scientific studies where people pray from a distance for the health and recovery of people they don't know personally.

The results from these studies have been mixed. A few studies found that people who are the focus of a series of prayers do slightly better (but it might be that other factors are causing the slight increase in recovery and health). A few studies found that people who are the focus of a series of prayers do not do any better than those who receive no prayers from the study participants (but it's very unclear whether it was the specific prayers or other factors that are causing the mixed results regarding recovery and health).

For over 25 years, I've been watching these numerous scientific attempts that claim to be assessing whether prayer is effective or not at helping people heal. To be honest, I (and many other people in the social sciences, in medicine, and among spiritual and religious scholars) find these particular studies to be clumsily designed and probably unreliable. Whether you personally believe that prayer is helpful or not helpful, you have to scratch your head and wonder, "Why are these scientists asking volunteers who don't know very much about the person being prayed for, and possibly don't care all that much about the individual being prayed for, to be the 'scientific proof' of whether there is a compassionate Presence in the universe and whether prayer is helpful?"

To my mind, it seems a bit goofy that every few years there is another "Breaking News" press release from a big university research department that generates attention-grabbing headlines in newspapers and TV shows with flashy promises of "New Scientific Breakthrough Results" saying either that "This proves God exists" or "This proves God doesn't exist" based on a few hundred volunteers saying disconnected prayer words for people they don't know or care about very much. I would much rather say honestly and authentically, "This is one of the mysteries of life that we aren't going to prove or disprove with a simple study of a few hundred volunteers in remote locations uttering words that don't come from the heart."

So in this chapter on "What Happens When You Pray for Healing," I am not going to attempt to make any press-release or headline-grabbing declarations that "Science has suddenly found the ultimate proof!" Nor will I be running experiments where people say scripted words for a remote stranger they will never meet or embrace.

Rather, I am going to explore a "let's see what we have so far and let's not jump to any global conclusions" regarding exactly what does happen for the people who say sincere prayers and for the people who are on the receiving end of passionate prayers for healing. Does something shift? Does something improve? Does nothing happen? Are there clues that the effort spent praying can lead to something beneficial and noticeable?

Here's what we can say with some certainty about the usefulness (or lack of usefulness) of prayers for healing:

The First Thing That Often Happens

If you watch closely your emotions and your mental thoughts when you are praying for a loved one, and you watch closely the emotions and mental thoughts of the individual who is being prayed for, you will probably notice that quite often the first immediate outcome of the prayers is that your mood shifts a little from a state of fear and frozenness to a renewed sense of hope and openness. It feels rather profound to stop for a moment and to say honestly (out loud or silently), "I absolutely care about this individual. I want the best for this person and I am open to whatever can be helpful. I am willing to stretch outside of my comfort zone to help, to ask for guidance, and to brainstorm on options. I am not going to give up on this person. This is important and I am hoping my love and these words connect me with some useful steps I can take." A prayer sometimes opens up a channel for good ideas and helpful options to emerge.

It also feels rather profound when you are dealing with an ailment to find out that people near and far who care about you and love you are saying prayers for you. It's certainly a lot more uplifting and inspiring than being forgotten or being ignored. When you hear that someone is sincerely praying for your health and well-being, it often makes you stop and say, "Wow. Is this really happening? These individuals that know me well are saying prayers for my recovery and my comfort. This is a new experience for me, and it makes me want to go forward with an increased sense of strength and support."

Even if the person you are praying for is very ill and the doctors are citing statistics that say, "It's not looking very hopeful at all," the prayer for healing is saying "there's a lot more happening here than just statistics—there's a unique soul and that soul deserves our love, our support, and our creative ideas and teamwork right now on how to deal with this situation." It's somewhat like breathing additional oxygen in a room where there wasn't much oxygen—and when you breathe a little more oxygen your brain has a much better chance of coming up with good ideas for what possibilities might help reduce the various discomforts and improve the chances for gaining an additional boost of energy.

There is a very basic Jewish concept that is being activated each time you or I say a prayer for healing for ourselves or for someone we love. In Judaism, it is often stated that, "Where there is breath and where there is life, there is still the possibility of something holy happening here."

To understand what this means in real-life situations, many Jewish scholars, teachers, rabbis and pastoral counselors have written or spoken on the topic of "Being Realistic While Also Keeping Hope Alive." For example, a wonderful teacher I studied with several years ago, Rabbi Amy Eilberg from Philadelphia (who was the first female rabbi ordained in Conservative Judaism and was one of the founders of the Jewish Healing Center in San Francisco) has given many workshops on how to find the balance between, "When is the right moment to offer a hopeful suggestion, when is the right moment to admit there are now fewer options, and when is the right moment to just listen with an open heart and a warm presence?"

To spark your own thoughts about the dilemma of "realistic hope" versus "unrealistic hope," here are Rabbi Amy Eilberg's own words:

"As long as there is life, there is hope. On the other hand, it's not helpful to encourage unrealistic expectations on the level of physical healing, lest the patient and loved ones feel betrayed and shattered when this hope proves unjustified. Yet there are things to hope for, and an attitude of hopefulness is possible even in dark times."

Some of the hopeful things that sincere prayers for healing can stir up in us and our loved ones are:

A Renewed Closeness Between People Who Have Drifted Apart. If geographic distance or an unresolved disagreement have caused two people to lose touch or grow slightly cold toward each other, something transformative often occurs when one of them is seriously ill or in need of support. The prayers we say for healing often become the vehicles for opening up our hearts again and remembering how much this person means to us. Quite often the words of prayer soften the hurts we have been carrying and allow us to be there for each other once again.

Has that been true for you or someone you know? Has an illness or any prayers for healing ever caused you and some other person in your life to become just a little more forgiving or understanding toward each other? Has a prayer for healing ever caused you to say to yourself, "Maybe I'm ready to call this person on the phone or visit this person. Maybe there's hope that the two of us can be there for each other again (even in a small but meaningful way)."

A Hopeful Sense of Creative Brainstorming and Teamwork. I have also noticed in some families, some workplaces, and some circles of friends that an illness and prayers for healing occasionally (not always) spark a sense of teamwork, creativity, and shared purpose. Even if this particular family, this workplace, or this circle of friends has been going along for months or years with little sense of shared purpose or passion, the jolt of an illness sometimes turns into a concerned response from one or more individuals who then find a new sense of flexibility and motivation to be of service. These concerned individuals sometimes rally and share ideas on how each person can contribute to the urgent situation in a constructive way.

For instance, I remember several years ago one of my colleagues, a very brilliant and compassionate woman named Arlene, who had no family support, no current partner, and not very much savings or cash flow, had a medical crisis that caused six of her friends from various parts of her life to brainstorm together (at a lunch we arranged at a nearby restaurant and then with weekly teamwork phone calls, texts, and emails) on how each of us could help her situation. The six of us didn't know each other well before that quickly-arranged lunch, but from then on we became a "team" who brainstormed together consistently and helped our mutual friend deal with all the complicated aspects of her medical nightmare.

At moments like that, a prayer for healing is not just a message to God to "please fix this situation," but also a reminder of the important teamwork it takes to get things done in this world. We can ask for help from the Creative Source, but we are also asking ourselves during these prayers, "What is the teamwork and the caring I can give on this earthly plane of existence to help this person I care about—without causing burnout to my own health, but without doing less than I could honestly do." In Judaism, prayer is not usually just a passive act of

"Please God, do all the work for me while I sit here and say words of prayer," but rather a call to action and creative brainstorming because prayer often boosts the energy and the constructive ideas and involvement of the individuals who are saying the prayer.

A Feeling of Openness and Hope that There are Still More Alternatives Than the One That Hasn't Been Working. Sometimes when we are ill or a loved one is ill, we feel drained physically and emotionally, or we feel as if we've run out of possible solutions. But then in the middle of a prayer for healing, a renewed burst of insight and a renewed creativity emerges. Suddenly there is one more alternative, or several more possibilities, or some specific fine-tuning steps that can either improve things, or bring comfort and a reduction of suffering or isolation. Once again, the prayer for healing is not only calling out to the mysterious Source of Compassion and Strength. It's also waking up a part of ourselves that has felt drained or exhausted, yet the prayer lifts up our energy and asks, "Is there something I can do today or this week that will be helpful, caring, or comforting in this difficult situation? Is there some additional or uncharted way that needs to be explored even though I don't have all the answers?"

Here's a quick example of someone who experienced a substantial dose of hope and renewed creativity each time he prayed for health or he heard about friends and loved ones who were praying for his health:

I have a close friend named Glenn who during his 30's was a very-talented music company department head enjoying his career and his excellent relationship with his pregnant wife, when suddenly he was told that his Stage 4 metastatic lymphoma (that had spread to several organs in his body) was so serious and so beyond treatment that he should expect he has just six to nine months to live.

That hope-crushing prognosis from his highly-regarded doctor was 30 years ago and when I spoke on the phone with Glenn a few weeks ago, he recalled, "I was so terrified that my life was over and that my kid was going to grow up without a dad. But what kept me going all these years is that I knew people were praying for me. I'm not a very emotional person or very spiritual, yet there was something so uplifting and so hopeful about the fact that people cared enough to say words of prayer on my behalf and to offer their help in so many other ways. Knowing that I was not forgotten or dismissed made a huge difference and it helped me stay focused on constantly researching different clinical trials, various alternative approaches, and important lifestyle and nutrition improvements that I believe have helped a lot. Every day when I think about the people who prayed for me then and are still praying for me now, I feel a much stronger urge to do my part and to keep finding new options and specific steps that I bring to my doctors and help make sure they are paying attention to my complicated situation. Sometimes my lymphoma is quiet for a few months or a few years, and sometimes it flares up and scares the heck out of all of us. But the prayers and the sense of support I keep receiving from people in my life have kept me on track one day at a time, one month at a time, one year at a time for more than 30 years."

In a few weeks, Glenn will be dancing at his son's wedding. They have a very close father-son friendship and I'm in awe of how Glenn has been able to juggle all the difficult medical procedures while still being a caring and very-involved parent.

Please note that I am not saying with this brief story about my friend Glenn that every medical situation can be fixed by prayer and that prayers will somehow make all the symptoms go away. Glenn still has a lot to deal with medically each year and I have seen many,

many good and decent human beings who have said passionate prayers but were unable to overcome the fragility of our human bodies and the aggressive ailments that were more intense than even the most-sincere prayers and remarkable medical treatments could reverse.

Instead, what I am saying with Glenn's brief story is that sometimes if one or more people are praying for us, it not only might be having an impact on levels of existence we don't fully understand as humans, but it definitely can boost the hopefulness, the daily focusing, and the creative insights that might be helpful to the person who is ailing and to the caregivers who also need a burst of renewed hopefulness every so often. We never fully know just how much a caring conversation, a supportive listening moment, or a prayer for strength or guidance can improve a situation and bring out the best in people. But in Glenn's case, he not only is aware of how much the prayers of others have meant to him emotionally, but also how they have helped him to be so persistent and unrelenting in looking for additional methods and treatment options that he was able to bring to his doctors to increase his chances of being alive all these years.

What Else Happens When We Pray for Healing: Your Choice for the Translation of an Important Word Can Make a Big Difference in How You Feel About Your Life Each Day

Now we get to something very interesting and very practical about the Jewish prayer for healing. The traditional Hebrew prayer for healing, the Mee Sheh-bay-rakh, can be translated in two very different ways. Consider this for a moment:

Translation #1: May the One who blessed our ancestors, now bring blessings and healing to this individual (either your own name or the name of someone you are concerned about) with a renewal of spirit and a renewal of body, and a refu-ah sh'laymah, **a complete healing.**

Or Translation #2: May the One who blessed our ancestors, now bring blessings and healing to this individual (either your own name or the name of someone you are concerned about) with a renewal of spirit and a renewal of body, and a refu-ah sh'laymah, **a healing toward wholeness.**

The word "refu-ah" means healing or renewal. The word "sh'laymah" has the same root as the familiar word shalom (wholeness, peace, the harmonious working together of the many different parts). Your choice of whether to translate refu-ah sh'laymah as "a complete healing" or "a healing toward wholeness" might not sound at first like a big difference, but in fact it can cause you to feel either like you are doing an excellent job on your healing journey or that you are failing miserably on your healing journey. Here's what I mean:

If you ask God, or the universe, or your medical providers for "a complete healing," you are essentially saying, "I probably won't be satisfied or feel good about the progress we are making unless we hit that perfect target of 100% removal of symptoms and 100% return to the highest level of functioning that I ever experienced." More importantly, if you have a chronic condition, or a complicated ailment or medical challenge that has recurring issues that need to be managed carefully even while you are making substantial progress, then the all-or-nothing request for "a complete healing" might feel as if you are constantly failing or getting a less-than-adequate answer to your prayers.

Quite often I have seen counseling clients, friends, and relatives who have chronic conditions such as MS (multiple sclerosis), or back and shoulder discomforts, or certain kinds of immune system vulnerabilities, or occasional seizures, or specific allergies, or occasional flare-ups of depression and anxiety, or occasional flashbacks from past traumas, and when they pray for "a complete healing" they invariably end up feeling, "What unfortunately am I doing wrong that I still have more stuff to deal with. I wish I could be 100% better and, as a result, I get upset each time I am reminded that I'm not 100% done with all this."

Praying for a 100% removal of symptoms is a bit like my closing my eyes and praying passionately to not be bald. What?? Does it really make sense for me to be asking to have the hair of Harry Styles or Keanu Reeves? It's a free country and we can pray for anything. But as to my request to "not be bald and to have a 100% complete healing," guess what happens. When I look in the mirror or see a photograph, I get to experience the disappointment that "this dude is definitely bald and my prayer was ineffective."

So if you have been praying for "a refu-ah sh'layma" for yourself or a loved one, and you were using the translation that it needs to be a 100% removal of all symptoms, complexities, and difficulties in order for your prayer to be effective, I can't stop you from translating the prayer that way.

But I am also hoping you will at least consider experimenting with the equally-valid translation #2 that asks for "a refu-ah sh'layma, a healing toward wholeness" or "a return to feeling whole again" that will spark good ideas which are a lot more practical, satisfying, successful, and constructive.

Here's what it means to pray for a refu-ah sh'layma that inspires you to open up to "a healing toward wholeness" or "a renewal of feeling whole again."

- It means you are asking for the clarity to see yourself as a whole person once again (rather than a "damaged," "defective," or "less-than-whole" person because there are a few things for which you still need some support or assistance).

- It means you are not going to be as shocked or horrified each time on your healing journey that there are some occasional setbacks, detours, or mid-course corrections you need to make in order to stay as healthy and productive as possible.

- It means you can feel good about each forward step you are taking to learn more, respond better, and come up with new ways to address what you are facing (rather than feeling discouraged or defeated because a particular medical condition has lots of twists and turns).

- It means you can be mindful and take good care of the delicate or vulnerable parts of your body without feeling ashamed or afraid to admit to others that you are not supposed to be "100% free of all vulnerabilities."

- It means you don't have to feel "weak" or less-than-whole when you say "no thank you" to some food, activity, or stressful situations that tend to drain your energy, or when you ask for understanding from someone who wasn't aware that your particular medical situation has some challenging aspects that need to be managed wisely.

Instead of being at war with your own body, and at war with God or the universe because you have a chronic condition or a sometimes-complicated health situation, from now on when you ask for a refu-ah sh'laymah as a "healing toward wholeness" you can take a gentle breath and have a moment of harmony and peace (sh'layma is that energizing feeling of harmony and peace).

Here's a quick and very personal example of how to successfully pray for a nourishing and uplifting "refu-ah sh'laymah, a healing toward wholeness," even when you are dealing with a quite challenging medical situation. Please see if this true story about my wife Linda gives you some ideas for your own health journey, or for the specific issues that one of your loved ones, friends, or colleagues is facing:

In early 2018, my wife Linda found out that she needed to have a major surgery in order to deal with a very aggressive, inflammatory, Stage 3 cancer that had put her health in danger and spread to her lymph nodes. In the first few weeks after the surgery, we were taking good care of the bandages and tubes that were part of the initial recovery process. But Linda was understandably worried about what was coming up in six more days when she would be seeing her new physical self for the first time because the post-surgical bandages and gauzes needed to be removed.

During the week before Linda would be taking off her bandages, she came up with a very original and interesting idea. She thought about creating a ritual that could help her approach with reverence her new body—to honor the surgery and sacrifice she had chosen in order to continue to experience life fully and to be open to some unexpectedly joyful and wonderful new chapters of her life from that time forward. She imagined asking two of her closest female friends to be there to help her take the bandages and gauzes off for the first time. She also began to write a special prayer about what this moment would mean to her.

Later that day, Linda decided to go forward with this idea, and she invited to our home on the next Sunday morning (the morning when the bandages could be taken off safely) two remarkable women she has known for many years. She phoned and asked them if they would be willing to help her create a new type of Jewish ritual for seeing one's body for the first time after a major surgery and connecting with a refu-ah sh'laymah, a healing toward feeling whole again.

Linda was a little nervous about asking for help from these two busy friends, but she felt reassured after she spoke on the phone with our beloved Rabbi Miriam Hamrell, who was very supportive, and with our longtime friend Janet Sternfeld Davis, who is a Talmud teacher at American Jewish University and who was very willing to participate in this new type of ritual. They both arrived at 10am on that Sunday morning and they were very open to hearing the spontaneous words Linda had written about what this moment meant to her (and what her hopes and concerns were for the future).

Before taking off the gauzes and bandages, they prayed together for strength and guidance for Linda's healing journey and they listened as Linda described the fact that she was not going to see herself as a passive victim, but rather was actively choosing to sacrifice some of what she had possessed physically in the past in order to be alive and enjoy each day in the future. With tears in their eyes, they talked about how hard it is sometimes to let go of our attachment to who we were before a health challenge and to be open to who we are now. They shared their strength and courage as women, so that this moment of taking off the bandages and seeing oneself in a new way could be holy and life-affirming.

As Linda described, "This ritual and support for taking off my bandages made the experience change from a dreaded situation and turned it into something that I will never forget, because I felt loved, cared for, and stronger than I expected I would be."

My wife Linda still has lots to deal with each day as a result of her ongoing medications and the after-effects from her cancer treatments. But her prayer that Sunday morning and her prayers ever since that day have been about saying yes to life and saying yes to the complicated journey of healing and wholeness. Each time we pray at services, or at a Shabbat candle-lighting, or in our quiet, silent moments for a refu-ah sh'layma, a healing toward wholeness, it feels as if we are gaining strength (and opening up to many levels of support and guidance) in order to stay sufficiently healthy and appreciate every sweet moment of life.

If you or a loved one are dealing with a serious ailment, or a recurring medical or psychological challenge, or a chronic condition that has ups and downs, please make sure you find a moment to write in your journal, or to talk with a supportive friend, rabbi, or counselor, about how to align your thoughts and your actions toward saying yes to healing, yes to being mindful, yes to feeling whole, and yes to life. That's what a healing prayer can do if we decide to say it with this deep intention.

One More Key Element of a Jewish Prayer for Healing: Reversing the Flow to a More Generous and Productive Direction

In the traditional, full version of the Mee Sheh-bay-rakh prayer for healing that you might read from a prayer book, or that you might hear a rabbi or a hospital chaplain say warmly at services or at someone's bedside, there is a surprising and unusual phrase. It says:

"May the One who blessed our ancestors, please bless and heal this person (you fill in your name or the name of the person you are concerned about) because (your name goes here) will contribute to charity on her/his behalf…"

You might be asking, "What's this? Why in the middle of a prayer for healing is there a mention of donating to charity? Is this some type of cosmic bribe?"

The answer to that question is quite profound and deep. In Judaism there is a recognition that this fragile and sometimes-broken world we live in is definitely in need of repair (tikkun olam—to repair the world) and that there are times when things seem to be flowing in a bad direction.

That's why in the prayer for healing, it essentially says, "Let's donate to a charity we care about and do our part to reverse or improve the direction of the flow."

If you think about it for a minute, that's a quite brilliant way to deal with a stressful or upsetting situation. Instead of falling into despair or a feeling of helplessness, the Mee Sheh-bay-rakh prayer is saying, "Right now, or later today, or first thing tomorrow, you have a perfect chance to do something constructive and useful with this person in mind. You can lift up your depleted energy and lift up the possibilities of healing in this fragile world by quickly giving something small or large to some folks who are working hard for healing, or for research, or for providing services to those who need it desperately. You are not helpless or powerless. You can do something immediately to improve the direction of the flow."

As you say or hear the Mee Sheh-bay-rakh prayer (or when you say your own spontaneous words for healing and renewal), imagine that your small or large donation to a charity is part of a steady flow of generosity and caring that is boosting the prospects for healing (not only for your loved one but for all sorts of individuals who are needing assistance right now). Maybe you will donate to some organization that directly helps people who are challenged by what you or your loved one is facing. Maybe you will donate to an organization that provides emotional support or excellent information and guidance for people and their loved ones who are facing tough decisions. Maybe you will make it possible for someone with limited funds to get quality care now, or to make it possible for crucial research to find improved medical options in the future.

By raising up your own worried mood and instead taking immediate action to give to a charity and help improve things near and far, your prayer for one person's healing becomes part of an enormous wave of good constructive energy in this fragile world. You are no longer a frightened, isolated victim of a tense medical situation. Now you are choosing to be part of the ongoing flow of improvement and repair. That's how the Mee Sheh-bay-rakh prayer raises us up to the possibility of turning this current challenge into a spontaneous opportunity for something good and holy to happen.

As you think about your own medical challenges or the challenges that a loved one is facing, is there one particular charity or group that you can contribute to with an "In Honor Of" note that can boost the healing journey that you or a loved one are on right now? You can be cynical and call it a cosmic bribe. Or you can be realistic and call it a chance to turn one aspect of the world in a good direction because your heart has been opened by the medical realities you are facing.

I hope that when you send the check or hit the "Pay Now" button for the credit card donation, that you can appreciate how much your act of lovingkindness is going to help many individuals and their loved ones now and in the future.

The Specific Prayer That Helped Me Go Under the Knife

To end this chapter, I want to complete the unanswered question that was raised at the beginning of the chapter. You might recall I mentioned in the opening paragraph that when the nurse was about to give me the knock-out fluids for my sudden surgery, I said a prayer. Well, here's the prayer I sang silently and it's one of my favorite prayers for healing:

The last line of the Adon Olam prayer that many congregations sing at the end of services and that many people say at bedtime or before a medical procedure has these words:

"B'yado af-keed roo-khi, b'eit ee-shahn v'ah'eerah

V'eem roo-khi g'vee-yah-tee, Adonai lee v'loh ee-rah."

Which can be translated as:

"Into God's hands I entrust my spirit, when I sleep and when I wake;

and with my spirit, my body also: Adonai is with me, I will not fear."

Or in the beautiful melodic version written by singer-songwriter Craig Taubman (that can be sung solo or as a comforting and uplifting duet) it is translated as:

"My soul I give to you, my spirit in your care.

Draw me near, I shall not fear, hold me in your hands.

Draw me near, I shall not fear, safely in your hand."

If you take a breath and listen calmly to this particular version, the melody feels like a soothing lullaby for letting go of fear when you are worried or concerned about undergoing a complicated medical procedure. I know lots of Jewish individuals of all ages (and all levels of belief or doubt) who have told me, "This is the specific prayer that got me to relax and trust, so that I could let these health care professionals do what they are trained to do, even if I am a bit of a control freak and I am definitely not in control at that moment of going into surgery." One of my friends, a tough but tender guy, originally from Brooklyn, named Michael Stevens, actually sang this version out loud to the nurses giving him anesthesia as he went in for a major operation.

While on one level this prayer about "hold me safely in your hands" is a gentle lullaby, on another level it has a profound intellectual component. If, just for a moment, we quickly analyze the last line of the Adon Olam, you might find it interesting that there are at least three different Jewish ways to understand the word "hands" or "hand" when we say we are entrusting our body and spirit into someone's hands. Here, very briefly, are three different ways to think about what is meant by "hands." See which ones you resonate with and which ones are not your cup of tea:

Option #1: That Human Hands Are the Indications of a Higher Presence.

Some Jews and some rabbis agree with Rabbi Harold Kushner, the author of "When Bad Things Happen to Good People," and many other modern rabbis and scholars who suggest that we live in a world where there is a lot of randomness built into creation and many things that are still chaotic and uncertain (and in Kushner's view, even God cannot control some of these random elements that are built into the ongoing flow of life and they get unleashed at times). Yet Kushner and many other rabbis suggest that how we choose to respond to chaotic moments is what truly matters, and that God's love and presence is revealed through the care and commitment of doctors, nurses, caregivers, family members, friends and other helpers who transmit God's healing energies on Earth. In other words, the caring people we have in front of us during a medical procedure are "God's hands" and the prayer for "being safely in Your hands" beautifully aligns us with those caring transmitters of Divine support.

Option #2: That We Are Asking for a Direct Intervention from a Higher Source.

Some Jews and some rabbis agree with the more traditional view of God as an all-powerful force who can intervene in any situation. Among religiously-observant Jews you often hear the phrase, "B'ezraht Ha-Shem (with God's help)," which refers to the belief that our human efforts are in our hands, but that the ultimate outcome of a situation is in God's hands and according to God's mysterious will. In other words, when you or I say the words "safely in your hands" (and if we believe a little or a lot in the traditional perspective of asking for God's immediate assistance), we are essentially conversing directly to the Creative Source and asking for the Source of Healing to intervene immediately (like Moses asked God to heal his sister Miriam when Moses called out, "Eil nah, refa-nah lah, Please God heal her now").

Option #3: That We Are Connecting with a Compassionate Presence Which Expresses in All Sorts of Ways.

If you think about the Hebrew word Ha-Rakhaman (one of the many names for God), which has two simultaneous meanings, (Ha-Rakhaman can be translated as "The Compassionate One" and it also means "the womb of life,") you can immediately start to envision and connect with a caring womb of elements that are going to get you through this surgery or this medical challenge.

For instance, in a hospital you might be hooked up with some machines that are helping you with oxygen and monitoring your heart rate, your blood pressure, your sodium levels, and other vital signs. In that moment of saying a quiet prayer, the "hands" that are supporting you might look like a cold machine, an oxygen tube, or an intravenous drip, but in fact those devices have sources of power which come from the electrical grid that comes from the sun, the hydroelectric water sources, and the hydrogen, oxygen, and other molecules which all were created by the Source of Creation and that surround us daily like a giant nourishing womb of life.

In addition, the batteries in those machines that are helping you breathe and stay stable in your heart rate, sodium levels, and blood pressure have natural minerals such as nickel, cobalt, lithium, graphite, cadmium and other natural elements that come from the Creative Source and were put into the Earth with endless possibilities for generating clean energy (if they get recycled carefully).

Also, you might want to consider the fact that the doctors, nurses, and aides are keeping the incision clean and their hands clean (and keeping you free from dangerous infections) each time they wash with iodine, isopropyl alcohol, aloe, clean water, and other mixtures of natural chemicals that come from the Earth and from a Creative Source whose "womb of life" provides us with abundant possibilities for healing in safe, infection-preventing ways.

You are not alone and unsupported as you go into surgery or some other medical procedure. The womb of life-sustaining minerals, chemicals, plants with healing properties, as well as the specific inventions, innovative devices, research discoveries, and caring individuals that are part of your medical procedure (all of them created or inspired by a Source that is beyond our human understanding) are there with you. Not only is the Creative Source found in all these life-affirming elements, but you can also find a hint of the Divine in the still small voice within you that might be whispering, "It's okay to go forward with this. It's okay to breathe and relax. Inhale, exhale. One calming breath at a time."

The next time you or a loved one are going for a medical procedure, or you are doing something healing or reparative on your own at home, you as a Jew get to decide whether you believe that your support at that moment comes from human hands, Divine hands, an abundant womb of life from a mysterious Source, or a combination of two or three of these possibilities.

As I was singing silently to myself (I am not as courageous or bold as my dear friend Michael Stevens who sang out loud in the hospital pre-op room), I began to relax somewhat as I remembered that there are helpful sources of healing (and possibly an Infinite Source of Healing) all around us and that a successful outcome is quite possible.

I hope and pray for good outcomes for you and your loved ones, too. We are all fragile and we are all in need of healing sooner or later. Please make sure to never stop asking and never stop exploring in your search for healing in whatever form healing is still possible.

CHAPTER SIX:

How the Kaddish Works
on Many Levels

What has been your personal experience with the rhythmic prayer that starts with "Yit-gahdahl v'yit-kahdahs or "Yis-gahdahl v'yis-kahdahsh?" When you first heard those words at a funeral or a congregational service, did it make you curious as to why the people around you were treating it with so much reverence and importance? Is it something that has ever brought tears to your eyes or a warm feeling in your heart when you said it for a loved one who is no longer on Earth? Has the Kaddish prayer ever seemed confusing to you—a bit of a mystery as to why it stirs up so many feelings and memories, or what it actually means, or how it works?

For me, the Kaddish prayer is both a mystery and a longtime source of comfort. When I was fourteen and my mom died, I felt sad and exhausted from four and a half years of daily efforts (along with my dad and my sister) to keep my mom alive, dealing with all sorts of setbacks, and then watching her slip away.

At the funeral, I saw my beloved immigrant grandparents crying repeatedly for their very smart and devoted daughter that they never expected to have to bury at a young age. I wondered if they would ever be able to get beyond the pain of losing her.

On the day after the funeral, one of my nicest relatives, a very caring and highly-intelligent aunt, took me aside and gently explained to me that I might want to think about going to services in the next year as often as possible to say the Kaddish in order to help my mother's soul be elevated on its journey.

"Elevating her soul?" I had no idea what that meant. At that young age, I had only a vague notion of what a "soul" is. To be honest, because I was growing up in Detroit, I associated the word "soul" with Aretha Franklin, Marvin Gaye, Gladys Knight, and Otis Redding. On the radio, one of my favorite songs was Otis Redding belting out slowly and passionately:

"I've been lovin' you-oo-oo-oo-oo,

too-oo lon-on-on-on-on-ong,

To Stop Now!"

A few days later at Sabbath services, as I stood with tears in my eyes saying the ancient words "Yit-gahdahl v'yit-kahdahsh…" in a room filled with people much older and more fluent in saying the Kaddish prayer than I was, I remember thinking, "Maybe that's what the Kaddish is trying to say to me. That I've been loving her for far too long to stop now." The melodic sounds of the "Yit-gahdahl v'yit-kahdash" seemed to be whispering, "It's okay to still feel all that love and connection. It's okay to drift in and out of these intense thoughts and emotions that most of the other mourners at these same services are also feeling. Even though she's no longer on Earth, you can feel somehow connected to her when you say these holy ancient words."

So, for the next twelve months and at various times every year since that extremely-confusing first year, I've been thinking about my mom's complicated life and loving her through the ritual of saying the words of the Kaddish prayer.

Has that ever happened for you? Is there someone you cared about passionately who left this earthly plane, but this person is very much alive in your heart and your thoughts when you say one of the Jewish memorial prayers?

In addition to my highly-intelligent aunt who gently encouraged me to do my part to say the Kaddish in order to help my mother's soul "be elevated," I also had been told by another of my relatives, a very well-educated and financially-successful cousin, that, "Jews used to believe in souls and the after-life, but most Jews today don't believe that stuff any longer."

As a teenager, I wasn't sure which of these two relatives to believe. They both seemed so convinced of their differing perspectives—one who was saying we are spiritual beings and that our beautiful souls live much longer than our fragile bodies, while the other was saying, "Nonsense! We don't believe in that stuff these days."

A Search for Answers

Over the past several decades, I've studied with many rabbis, teachers, mystics, scientists, researchers, and Jewish scholars about the several diverse ways of understanding the word "soul" in Judaism and what might happen for an expansive soul when it is no longer confined or tethered to a restrictive mortal body. I wanted to find out from a variety of Jewish and scientific perspectives if saying certain memorial prayers could possibly assist the journey of someone who died, or if that person simply lives on in our hearts but nowhere else. I wanted to explore whether when Jews today attend a funeral, or a Shiva gathering (seven days of mourning and support), or a Yizkor service (remembering our loved ones) at one of the holidays, are they just saying empty words or is there something more spiritual and important that might be happening.

This chapter is about what I've found regarding the controversial question for which my aunt and my cousin saw things quite differently in their two opposing points of view. Even today in the year 2022, there are many Jews who agree with my cousin and say, "There ain't nothing out there. When you're dead, you're dead." Yet there are an increasing number of Jews in the past few decades and in 2022 who agree with my aunt and say, "I'm curious. I'm interested in learning more. I don't have all the answers, but I have a sense that there is something about the soul that goes beyond the physical shell that housed it."

One thing I know for sure is that more and more Jews today are asking excellent questions about the human soul and the journey of a soul beyond this lifetime. For the past few years, I've been fascinated by the fact that several of my counseling clients and friends who are rabbis, pastoral counselors, or adult education teachers have each told me that thirty years ago if they tried to teach a course on "Jewish Views of the Soul and the After-Life," there would only be a few students showing up for the class. But in the past ten years, when they have announced a class or a reading/discussion group on the topic of "Jewish Views of the Soul and the After-Life," there was a much larger turnout and tremendous interest in the diverse ideas from Jewish teachings about what happens to our souls when we die.

What about you and your loved ones? Are the questions about what happens to our souls a topic that you've never quite broached with friends or family members? Or is it something that you've been curious about and have studied on your own, or in a class, or in a discussion group?

Whether or not you as an individual tend to feel moved by the Kaddish or curious about what happens when someone dies, I am hoping you will find some new insights and some new connection to this ancient prayer and these intriguing topics while you are reading the next several pages. I won't be telling you what to believe or how to practice, but I will be sharing with you some things that have made me slow down and say with a sense of wonder, "Wow, I never previously knew that particular interesting aspect of the Kaddish prayer. I wish someone had taught me that a long time ago."

How It Works on Different Levels

If you look it up on Google, you will find there are hundreds of articles about the Kaddish prayer and why even Jews who don't believe in God still tend to say the Kaddish prayer and feel moved by it. If you go to Amazon.com or Books in Print, you will find there are dozens of books, many of them from famous and beloved authors, about their personal experiences of saying the Kaddish for a loved one. Two of my favorites are "Mourning and Mitzvah" by Rabbi Anne Brener, who was trained as a social worker and psychotherapist before studying to become a rabbi, and "Saying Kaddish" by Anita Diamant, who has written excellent books on how to put together a Jewish wedding, how to celebrate and raise a Jewish child, and her bestseller "The Red Tent" about a horrific incident in the Torah.

These two extremely-useful books about the Kaddish (along with the numerous articles and books by other authors about this intriguing prayer) sometimes disagree about specific details or diverse beliefs, but they all say one agreed-upon truth about the ancient ritual that starts with "Yit-gahdahl v'yit-kahdahsh:" They each say that it is a profound and unforgettable moment when you say the Kaddish prayer from the heart and you have a wave of memories about a loved one who is gone from this Earth.

How exactly does the Kaddish stir up so much emotional impact and healing for so many diverse individuals year after year, century after century? Here, very briefly, are four different reasons why scholars, writers, teachers, rabbis, and everyday folks suggest that understanding more about the many levels of the Kaddish can be beneficial to you and your loved ones. See which of these four levels of understanding stir up something useful in your own thoughts and feelings, and which of these four levels might be useful for someone you know (who is grieving for a loved one or is curious about the mysteries of life):

Beneficial Kaddish Exploration #1: That You or I Can Walk into Almost Any Service Anywhere in the World and Feel Connected to the Empathy and Understanding of So Many Other Jews Who Have Said This Same Prayer with Deep Emotion

I love traveling to places where the Sabbath services sound a little different because of local languages or local accents. The Hebrew you hear at a service in Israel (or in London, or in Paris, or in Montreal, or in Mexico) sounds a little different from the Hebrew at a service in my original hometown of Detroit (where our Michigan accents have a nasal "A" sound even when we are saying Hebrew words like shalom). Or when the Hebrew and English words sound a little different when I visit relatives in Pittsburgh (where the accents sound almost like the Philadelphia, Harrisburg, Baltimore, or Washington D.C. accents, but slightly different), or when I have gone to services in Texas or Georgia (where the "shalom y'all" has a unique sound), or when I pray in California (where the clothes are more casual and the Torah discussions are far more touchy-feely than when I've visited various congregations in New York, Boston, or Connecticut).

But at each of these diverse locations, there is one prayer that sounds almost exactly the same and feels very familiar no matter what time zone you are in. It's the Kaddish and if you happen to be away from home and you want to go to services to say Kaddish for one or more loved ones, you can walk into all sorts of congregations around the world and hear the recognizable "Yit-gahdahl v'yit-kahdash" or the "Yis-gahdahl v'yis-kahdash" (if it is a traditional Ashkenazic congregation with Eastern European pronunciations).

Many scholars suggest that the Kaddish was written intentionally to create a sense of "home" and "familiarity" for those who would be saying it. As a brief bit of history, you might know already that the Kaddish prayer wasn't written in Hebrew, but rather in Aramaic which was the mother tongue of numerous nations in the Middle East for many centuries from the 6th century before the common era and for 1300 years more until the 7th century of the common era (and even today in some Middle Eastern and Asian countries like Kurdistan where Aramaic is still spoken daily). The ancient rabbis decided to say this deeply personal memorial prayer in the familiar, comfortable Aramaic language that congregants of that time would speak intimately to their loved ones, rather than in the Hebrew words that many individuals didn't understand as easily.

It's a prayer where everyone in the room (even if they walked in that day as a new person who doesn't know anyone) is fully included as a compassionate support-team member for those who are mourning or who are filled with memories of a departed loved one. Has that ever happened for you? Have you ever started saying the Kaddish prayer in a room filled with people you don't know very well and then suddenly the rhythmic sounds of the "Yit-gahdahl v'yit-kahdahsh" opened up a wave of memories or feelings inside you that allowed you to be vulnerable and real among people who were also being open, vulnerable and real (sometimes with tears in their eyes)?

I remember in the Fall of 2016, my beloved father died. I was away from home to help with his burial in South Florida and it happened to be on the day before Rosh Hashanah, the Jewish New Year. Part of me wanted to fly home immediately after the burial to attend High Holiday services with the congregation that I have known and loved for many years. But a part of me wanted to stay a few more days in Florida to comfort my stepmom. I decided to call a local rabbi who was kind enough to let me come to her congregation in South Florida so that I wouldn't miss Rosh Hashanah that year. But I was concerned that I wouldn't know anyone else at that congregation and I wondered if I would feel like an uncomfortable outsider.

Those feelings of "aloneness" disappeared when I stood up to say the Kaddish and there were dozens of other mourners standing up as well, along with hundreds of supportive, caring faces sending us love and strength (even though we had never spoken a chatty word to each other).

As I recited the ancient, profound Aramaic words of the Kaddish in unison with all the other mourners around me, I was not "away from home." I felt "truly home and welcomed," being comforted by each of these Jews I had never met, yet we all shared a familiar prayer and an amazing sense of "we're in this complicated journey of life, death, and uncertainty together."

The next time you are in a prayer service and the Kaddish is being recited, look in front of you, behind you, and to the right and left for a moment and see what it means to you to be surrounded by individuals who (to some extent) know the profound experience of praying for a Jewish soul that we have loved. We might have different views about all sorts of issues, but there you are in a room full of Jews you might not know personally and yet there is something that causes you to feel "like family (in the good sense)" with these individuals (who are saying "Amen" at various points in the prayer to show their support for those who are grieving). The next time you say the Kaddish prayer with people you don't know all that well, see if you can experience something surprisingly comforting because you are each individual Jews from a variety of places and backgrounds, who are nonetheless connecting as one unified, supportive gathering to appreciate the love that each of you are feeling at that moment for particular individuals who are no longer living.

So, on one basic level, the Kaddish works as a profound piece of history, community, and shared emotion—a way to experience that you are not alone in your pain or grief, but you are surrounded by people who have an openness to what you are going through as you slowly heal from the loss of a loved one.

Beneficial Kaddish Exploration #2: That the Kaddish Prayer Can Help Us See at the Same Time Both the Cherished Departed Individual and Also the Big Picture of Exquisite Life Force and Future Possibilities.

It's normal for people to feel somewhat closed down or cut off from the flow of life when they're in grief or when their routines have been shaken up because a significant person in their life is suddenly gone. That sadness and that sense of "life feels different and a bit disoriented right now" can cause us to lose sight of everything else that is beautiful and energizing. When someone you love is no longer available on the phone or in person, you might be feeling a bit raw or unable to focus (with a sense of "I have a list of things that need to get done but lately I can't seem to stay on track or stick to anything.") You start to wonder if this sense of un-ease and feeling out of synch with the flow of life is going to last forever, or that your ability to feel productive and alive again might never return.

That's why on the level of personal healing, the chance to say the Kaddish prayer a number of times each month or each year is so remarkable and helpful. It seems to open up a new computer window inside your mind that can focus clearly on two completely different visual possibilities at the exact same moment (rather than being stuck with only one sad screen only). The Kaddish prayer helps your thoughts and your emotions to envision BOTH the person you are sad about and also the big picture of life in its fullness and awesome possibilities. Here's what I mean:

Imagine yourself standing up and saying or hearing the somber sounds of the "Yit-gahdahl, v'yit-kahdahsh" words of the ancient Aramaic prayer that has you remembering the person you love who is no longer here on Earth, while at the same time the English translation of the Kaddish is saying essentially, "There is still some light emerging in this world and right now you can add a second possibility to what you are seeing at this unique moment. There is still some goodness in this world and you can add an awareness that there is still a lot to celebrate about this world we are living in. Definitely, there is an amazing abundance of beauty in nature and creation, many future adventures and possibilities that will emerge when you are ready to re-enter the flow of life, and frequent acts of human kindness and helpful support which are also true, even when we are feeling sad or missing someone. There is an awesome flow of caring and connection that surrounds you right now. It's only a few breaths away."

The actual translated words of the Kaddish prayer are about praising and once-again noticing the vast Creative Source, the endless Life Force, that is still pulsing strongly and constantly at this very moment (and you can sense this unstoppable Life Force in the winds, the ocean tides, the spectrum of colors, the acts of human lovingkindness, the creative ideas and intuitive wisdom in our brains, and the heart pulse and breathing within our own bodies). The Kaddish prayer translation says that this Creative Source, this nourishing Life Force, is giving us blessings, support, and possibilities for healing and connection, even during a moment when we are filled with complicated memories of sadness or loss, or when we are feeling cut off from the flow of life.

The Kaddish prayer doesn't say, "Don't be sad" or "Don't grieve," but rather it allows us to be sad and grieve with one eye (or one computer window section inside your mind), while simultaneously seeing on an additional computer window section inside your mind that this world is awesome in many, many ways and that the Creative Flow is still very much alive. When you say the Kaddish, you are standing up and honoring the terrible loss you feel (as you memorialize someone you love) at the same time that the rhythmic words of the Kaddish are saying essentially, "There is a beautiful, complicated world and a need for all of us to work for peace and goodness as soon as we are ready to get back into action. Let the Kaddish give you energy for healing and a vision to keep going forward. And let us say Amen."

That might not be easy or automatic for you or a loved one to do. Sometimes our brains lock onto one painful sad memory and we can't seem to notice much else at the same moment.

Here is a brief example of someone who was having trouble being able to see any light or any comfort after a very painful loss of a loved one. My friend and colleague Joni lost her beloved spouse as a result of a tragic car accident and she was in deep grief. Normally a very creative and productive person, Joni began to slip into lingering feelings of bitterness and discouragement, that would surround her with dark thoughts off and on during the first several months after the car accident.

One afternoon when we were talking on the phone about a number of topics, she said she wanted to ask a question about what it felt like for her when she said the Kaddish prayer. Joni admitted, "I'm not a very religious person, but I have gone a few times to say the Kaddish and to see what that's like."

My friend and colleague Joni (like many people when they are deep in grief) told me she felt somewhat confused and a little out of sorts with the English translation that was all about praising God, appreciating God's creation, and celebrating life and possibilities for peace and progress. Joni explained, "Right now I'm a bit frustrated with God and disconnected from the life I used to enjoy. It feels strange to be praising God and life when I'm in this state of discouragement."

I listened and I offered Joni my support for what she was going through. I could hear that she was beginning to let the tears flow and she needed someone to just be there on the phone and let her feel what she was feeling.

But then Joni took a breath and asked me a direct question. She said, "I know for a fact that you've had some painful losses and deep grief at several points in your life. Why do you think the Jewish memorial prayer is filled with so much praise and upbeat visions of the world? How come it's not sad, or cautious, or hesitant, when there is clearly so much loss and difficult stuff we all have to deal with?"

I thought for a moment and then replied, "I guess for me the Kaddish is a chance to realize that both sides of life are true and important. The love and sadness you and I feel for someone who is no longer alive is definitely important. At the same time, the beauty of plants and trees and the refreshing sound of flowing water, as well as the creativity and courage of people, plus the progress and healing that is possible, and the many decent, caring people in our lives—these are also important and worth noticing but so hard to include in our vision when any of us are in deep sadness. The Kaddish says, 'Let's appreciate all of it, the whole mixed picture of life in all its diversity—the sadness and the hopeful stuff.' For me, the Kaddish reminds my insides to look for both sides of life at the same time, so that we don't get excessively drunk on the sad feelings, or excessively drunk on the joyful memories. When we say the Kaddish, we somehow find the ability to be alive and centered in both the sadness and the joy."

The next time you are saying the Kaddish prayer, you can do what most people do and just focus on the memories you are having about someone who died. Or you can wrestle with the English translation and ask yourself, "Am I ready to start noticing again that there is a world of nature, beauty, creativity, and goodness that I can open up to when I'm ready and at the reasonable pace that feels comfortable after what I've been through." Or you can experiment with the idea of, "Can I see both the sadness in my heart and the awesome aspects of life and the Creative Source, all at the same time. Can I look at several screens in my mind's eye at once and realize they are each true one day at a time, one moment at a time."

Beneficial Kaddish Exploration #3: Saying These Words Out Loud Can Help You Discover and Embrace the Hard-to-Find, Pure Soul of Someone Who Was Sometimes Difficult or Unpleasant to Be With.

Now we come to a healing aspect of the Kaddish that very few people talk about, but it can bring tremendous breakthroughs and new insights to our lives if we know to look for it. It's about a specific question: How do we say the Kaddish (or should we say it at all) for a difficult or sometimes-abusive parent or sibling, or for a friend or lover who hurt us in the past, or for a spouse or ex-spouse who was sometimes insensitive, toxic, or unreliable? Is it appropriate (or not) to stand up and say these ancient words of prayer for a person who was at times very upsetting to you or to someone you care about?

Many years ago, when I was researching for one of my earlier books about how to heal painful relationships with parents, ex-spouses, or some other family member or friend who was hurtful at times, I went to the vast library of the American Jewish University (it was then called The University of Judaism) to see what the ancient and modern rabbis and scholars have said or written about this topic. I read dozens of book chapters, articles, sermons, and commentaries on the issue of "what to do about someone who was hurtful" and then I happened to find an obscure dissertation (tucked away in one of the many stacks of saved dissertations from new rabbinic scholars) that someone wrote where she directly researched and analyzed various rabbinic teachings on the question of "Is it a good idea to say Kaddish for a hurtful family member who died without cleaning up the unfinished business?"

I won't go into all the details, but I will say that I was deeply moved by this researcher's willingness to carefully explore this question and all the feelings of betrayal and sadness that happen inside of us when we think we can trust a certain family member or loved one, but this person ends up doing some very hurtful things to us or to other people. Should we stand up and say the Kaddish for someone with whom we have such unfinished business and so many painful memories?

Here's one possible way that the Kaddish can help you heal your uncomfortable feelings about a troubled or hurtful individual who did some insensitive things to you or someone else: In many Jewish teachings from the Kabbalah and from Rabbi Isaac Luria in the 16th

Century, there is a fascinating concept that each Jew (even a troubled or highly-imperfect Jew) has inside him or her a pure soul and sparks of holy light, but that for many deeply-wounded or defensive people the pure soul is hard to find because it is covered by layers of klippot (husks, shells, scar tissue, defensive posturing, harsh personality traits) that cover over and significantly block the light and the goodness in their deeply hidden, hard-to-find soul.

That means if you stand up and say the Kaddish for a departed family member, ex-spouse, or other person who was sometimes toxic or hurtful, you are basically saying to the universe (and to your own heart and your kishkas—your intestines) that this person's hard-to-find inner light and deeply hidden, pure soul is no longer blocked or concealed by layers of klippot (husks and coverings from the harsh personality traits or the defensive postures that they exhibited during their time on Earth). Rather, you are praying for the fact that this person's inner light and pure soul have been (to some extent) uncovered, freed-up, and opened-up to be part of the vast light and soul of the universe.

Whether you believe or not in the concept of souls and an after-life, you can simply look at the current reality that this problematic person is no longer trapped in his or her difficult layers of personality and behaviors. If you choose to say the Kaddish for this individual who was so important (and so painful) in your life, you are basically saying, "I choose now to see that this troubled individual had deep inside him or her some sparks of holy light that sadly were covered up and hard to find when this person was alive. I choose to look right now and see that those hidden sparks of light are visible more than they were before, and I want to raise up those sparks."

One of my counseling clients is a man who grew up with a very critical and quick-tempered dad who often took out his frustrations on his kids and his wife. My counseling client had spent years resenting his dad and feeling blocked in many areas of his life because of the stored-up anger and hurt from his childhood. Since this counseling client happened to be a somewhat-religious Jew who often said the Kaddish for his beloved mom and one of his older siblings who had died several years ago, he asked me one time during a counseling session, "Do you think I should be saying Kaddish for my abusive dad, or would that feel like a lie?"

Like many good people who aren't sure whether to say Kaddish for a hurtful family member, my counseling client didn't want to be fake or dishonest, especially with something as important as the Kaddish prayer. So we talked back and forth about the Yes and No options of whether to say Kaddish for this client's hurtful dad, and what it might feel like to be standing up at services and praising the universe and the Creative Source of Life with that sometimes-abusive dad's soul in mind.

After a few minutes of weighing the different options, my counseling client took a deep breath and told me, "I think I know what I'd like to do. I'm going to say the Kaddish and see if it feels like a lie or if it feels genuine."

While each individual person has the freedom to choose whether or not to say this ancient, sacred prayer in memory of a departed family member who was hurtful, in the case of my counseling client, it caused a bit of a breakthrough. As he explained to me the week after he said Kaddish for the first time for his dad, "I was standing up near the end of services and for a moment I stopped thinking about my father's harsh personality and his hurtful words. For a moment I could sense a glimpse of my father's wounded inner child, and especially his pure soul that was so squashed and covered over by all of the things that happened to him in his early years and caused him to be such a short-tempered bully and such a hurtful person. For a moment I was standing there connecting with the pure soul of my dad and it felt very good. I actually had a tear in my eye (and I'm not someone who tends to cry) and I felt a little bit of love for my dad's unique soul that was so injured and blocked by the circumstances of his life on Earth."

I can't guarantee that saying the Kaddish for a difficult person who has died will suddenly or gradually cause you to feel a glimpse of compassion or love for this person's hard-to-find pure soul. Each of us is different and it might be that what this person did to you or to someone else is beyond forgiving. The choice is yours to make, but if you do decide to experiment with saying the Kaddish for someone who had many layers of defensiveness and harshness, see if you can catch a glimpse of this person's pure soul and inner light being liberated from its oppressive coverings as you say the words of the Kaddish. Notice whether your heart, your thoughts, and your intestines feel some relief from discovering that the light that was contained in this person is no longer blocked or trapped under so much woundedness.

Beneficial Kaddish Exploration #4: Helping the Soul of Someone You Love Who Was Quite Wonderful and Who Might Be on a Mysterious Journey that We Don't Quite Understand

Now that we've discussed the possibility of helping to raise up the soul of an individual who was sometimes hurtful, what would you like to do about someone who was quite loving and decent most of the time during his or her lifetime and is now departed? Are you interested in doing something that might assist this person's soul on its journey?

Let's start by exploring what the word "journey" might mean from a Jewish perspective. Even though some of our family members and friends may have told us that, "Jews don't believe all that nonsense about souls and an after-life," in fact there is a fascinating set of speculations, beliefs, and research that you might find interesting if you are even a little bit curious about the question, "Do we have a soul and does that soul outlast the physical body?"

Several years ago, I read a book called "Jewish Views of the After-Life" by Simcha Paull Raphael that describes the many different ways that Jews have spoken about and written about death and the journey of our souls. He gives specific evidence from ancient writings, medieval writings, scientific writings, modern writings, and from the most current decades that there have been numerous Jewish ideas and theories about how the soul leaves the body and what the soul needs on its journey in order to connect with whatever is out there and whatever is next.

If, like most modern Jews, you were told by someone that Jews today don't speculate on the issue of souls and the after-life, you may want to brace yourself since the well-researched and eye-opening book by Simcha Paull Raphael might knock your socks off because of how many interesting and inspiring possibilities (for how a Jewish soul outlives the fragile body) have been discussed by credible, thoughtful, and well-regarded Jewish teachers and writers over the centuries. You can walk away from the book by Simcha Paull Raphael saying, "Wow, that is some excellent food for thought" or you might say, "Wow, what a bunch of speculation that I don't quite buy," or you can say, "Hmmm, I'm a little more open than I was before but still a bit hesitant." But you will definitely have a much richer sense of how interesting and thought-provoking these Jewish teachings and theories are for addressing the question, "Does the soul that lived in the body of your loved one have a continued light or wavelength that needs to be appreciated."

According to Raphael (who after writing his book became a trained rabbi, teacher, grief counselor, and rabbinic advisor to those who want to treat the dying and their grieving survivors with respect and wisdom), there are several reasons why Jews in the 21st century are more interested than ever in exploring the journey of the soul. Some of these reasons are:

- We are no longer as frightened as previous generations about discussing and asking questions about souls and what happens to our souls. Ever since Elisabeth Kubler-Ross wrote "On Death and Dying" and revolutionized the way that our society talks about death and helping someone transition to whatever is next, Jews have been in the forefront of making sure that doctors, nurses, hospice care workers, palliative care professionals, funeral home administrators, and others bring compassion and decency to these delicate conversations and practices.

- Many progressive and liberal Jewish communities are seeing a renewed interest in making sure that the body is treated with extra care and kindness after a person dies (using some of the compassionate practices that were mostly done in previous decades by very traditional Jews only) and that the soul of the person is prayed for in ways that previously were not emphasized in these more-progressive communities. More than ever before, I am hearing numerous examples in recent years of traditional Jews and non-traditional Jews who are working together and exchanging information about how to care for the body and the soul of a loved one with acts of lovingkindness that have been practiced for many centuries and are being updated to our current century.

• Many Jews today are interested and quite knowledgeable in the beliefs and practices of Eastern religions that discuss openly the possibility of souls outliving the body and how to assist a soul on its journey. As a result, many open-minded Jews today are once again exploring and going deeper into the numerous Jewish spiritual beliefs and practices about caring for a soul—including beliefs and practices that their parents or grandparents had been ignoring or dismissing.

(For a short and easy-to-read summary of Jewish views about the soul and the after-life possibilities, there is a well-written and quick version in Chapter 13 of Rabbi Anne Brener's book "Mourning and Mitzvah." You can explore a variety of interesting ideas and concepts while standing on one foot, in less than fifteen minutes, and then decide whether you are curious in learning more about the Jewish views regarding what happens to the soul when someone dies).

What the Science Reveals

One of the specific beliefs that some Jews believe (and other Jews dismiss) is the question of whether it's possible to feel the presence, or experience a moment of guidance, from the soul of a departed loved one. On this particular question, there is actually a lot of carefully-designed scientific research that clarifies just how many people alive today have had a moment (or more than one moment) when they felt that the soul of a loved one had visited them or spoken to them, or appeared in a night-time dream, or a day-time sense of subtle connection.

You might be rolling your eyes and saying, "No way. That's not real. It's just someone imagining something that isn't really happening."

I'm not going to tell you what to believe or what not to believe. My job is to give you some facts and some research results, so you can make your own decision. Here's what we know thus far:

- There have been hundreds of studies in the United States and other countries of what the scientists call "A Spontaneous ADC (After-death Communication)." Some of the studies have dozens of randomly selected volunteers, while other studies have thousands of first-hand accounts of After-death Communication reported by people from all walks of life and level of education and income.

- Overall, there is a wide range of data on the question of "What percentage of people today have experienced one or more incidents of sensing the presence or guidance from a departed loved one?" Some studies found that over 70% of people today have had one of those moments when they sensed the presence of someone who is no longer on Earth. Other studies found that only 20% of people today have had that experience. One researcher at a major university compiled and assessed the scientific validity of hundreds of studies of spontaneous after-death communications and then tossed out the studies that were clearly unreliable. This researcher concluded that the more reliable average from the most scientifically-valid studies among all these hundreds of studies is that "30-35% of people today are likely to have one or more After-death Communications during the course of their lifetime."

- If you aren't embarrassed to ask around in your circle of friends, relatives, and colleagues you might find a similar percentage of people who have felt a vague or clear sense that a departed loved one has been present for a moment or has given some guidance or support in some form.

While I can't prove that these "visits" or "spontaneous after-death communications" are real and not imagined, I see it slightly differently than a question of "prove it" or "dismiss it." When I hear a friend, a relative, a colleague, or a counseling client tell me that they felt the presence of someone who has departed, I just listen with curiosity. I sometimes admit that I have felt those moments on a few occasions myself—one time when a former writing partner (who had recently died) appeared at the foot of my bed early one morning and I sensed her saying something important that I have never forgotten. Was it real or was it my imagination? I can't prove it either way.

But what we can do as curious individuals living here on Earth is make a decision about what you personally feel is the most compassionate thing to do. Here's how I see the decision options:

- If there is even a 30% chance that the soul of a loved one is on a journey and that this soul might need to connect with you or be assisted by you, are you willing to do your part?

- Or if there is only a 1 percent chance that the soul of a loved one is on a journey and that this soul might need to connect with you or be assisted by you, are you willing to do your part?

For many, many centuries (and today as well) at Jewish funerals and at memorial services (Yizkor) during several of the annual holidays, there is a beautiful prayer and song called "Ayl Mahlay Rakhameem (O God full of compassion)," which has a fascinating line in it that says, "Let this soul find refuge for ever in the shadow of Your wings, and let this soul be bound up in the bond of eternal life."

As you think about that phrase and you speculate on your loved one whose soul might be seeking refuge in the wings of a Presence that is beyond our understanding, you don't have to prove whether there is something scientifically verifiable called a soul or an after-life. You only need to decide if you want to say "Yes" or "No" or "Maybe" to the choice of:

"If there is even the possibility of there being a soul and an after-life for this individual that I loved, do I want to do my part to help that soul find refuge, peace, and maybe even an eternal life?"

Or do I want to vote "No" and say, "I am not interested in being part of those concepts at all."

Please choose whatever is true for you. I will honor whatever you decide.

And if your answer is "Yes" or "Maybe" to the question of, "Am I willing to say a prayer for the soul of the person who died," then the next time you say the Kaddish, please take a moment to envision this individual's released soul moving toward or arriving in the wings of Ha-Rakhamahn (which can be translated as the endless flow of compassion or the vast womb of connected energy that exists on a level you and I cannot fully comprehend). Or you can envision this individuals' released soul moving toward or arriving in the wings of the Shekhinah, the In-dwelling Presence of the Endless Creative Source.

And if you are a skeptic or you're hesitant to believe in things like a soul and an after-life, please know that I am not asking you to ignore your skepticism. Here's a quick example of someone who was quite scientific, quite skeptical about religion, and quite willing to stretch a bit on behalf of a loved one:

Katrina is a brilliant medical researcher I have known for many years who told me once, "I only believe in things I can see with my own eyes (or the help of a microscope) and that I can verify with definitive scientific evidence." So, when Katrina lost her beloved younger sister and was invited to say the Kaddish at the funeral and at the gathering at her brother-in-law's house the next night, Katrina was hesitant.

When we talked on the phone a few hours before the funeral, Katrina explained to me, "I don't want to be a hypocrite and be saying things that aren't true." She was concerned that saying the Kaddish and trying to elevate the soul of her younger sister might imply that Katrina believed in concepts like "soul" and "after-life" that Katrina didn't believe and didn't want to pretend to believe.

I listened to Katrina and I could hear how much she was struggling with this dilemma. On the one hand, she wanted to assert her love of truth and scientifically-verifiable reality. On the other hand, she had been very close to her younger sister and she didn't want to do anything that might be harmful to that loving relationship or offensive to her sister's widower and the other grieving relatives.

So, I asked Katrina, "Is it okay to be definitely skeptical about things like soul and the after-life, but to be open to the remote chance that if there is even a one-tenth of one percent possibility that your sister has a soul that is seeking its next level, you have a little bit of openness to supporting that it goes well for her?"

Katrina thought for a moment and then said, "Well, in science we don't always have 100% proof. Quite often we have to settle for a statistical confidence level of 90% or 95% or 99% and we might say something is true but in fact there is still the small percentage of possibility that we are mis-reading the entire situation and something else is true."

Then she paused and commented, "As long as I still have the right to be skeptical and hesitant, then I'm okay with being a little bit open to the extremely remote possibility that there might be a one-tenth of one percent chance that my sister's soul needs me to pray for her. I can go with that."

As Katrina told me a few days later, "It felt good to be there with my sister's family and be saying the Kaddish with them. Yes, I'm a devoted scientist. But more than that, I am someone who cares about my sister and the grieving members of our extended family."

One of the things that is so beautiful about the Jewish community today and about being Jewish in the 21st century is that we can have different beliefs (and moments of skepticism, hesitance, and disagreement) and we are still embraced as being part of the community. So, the next time (if you are willing) that you stand up and say the Kaddish for a loved one, please don't think you have to pretend to be 100% in agreement or 100% sure that you believe with complete certainty that you are assisting the soul of the person you are praying for in a room full of mourners and supporters who are saying "Amen." You can honor your private truth (with all sorts of beliefs, questions, and doubts) and at the same time open up your heart and imagine your loved one possibly being raised up (however you envision that to be) by the ancient words "Yit-gah-dahl v'yit-kah-dash."

CHAPTER SEVEN:

How to Increase the Inner and the Outer Light

Have you ever looked closely at a candle flame and watched it dance? Whether you are 12, or 22, or 52, or 82, most of us get fascinated when we stop for a moment to watch the hot blue and white colors, along with the cooler red, orange, and grey hues jumping in the air and changing shape continually in a beautiful flame.

In Jewish homes, temples, and synagogues for many, many centuries, people of all ages have become enchanted and soothed by the light of candle flames that were lit with love and special meaning. It might be on a Friday night at home or at a congregational prayer service when the candles are lit at the start of the Sabbath. Or on Saturday night when a multi-wick flame emerges from the twisted braided candle of Havdalah (the moment when the sweet Sabbath is over but the glow from the Sabbath is carried in our hearts into the busy week ahead of us). Or at Hanukah when the colorful candles and songs light up the darkest time of the year. Or at various holiday gatherings during the year when the lighting of tall candles says to everyone in the room, "This is a special moment of togetherness. This light can connect us and inspire us at this time of year."

Do you have some personal memories of what it was like for you as a kid staring at the flame of a candle and feeling a sense of connection to something holy or mysterious? Even if you didn't grow up in a family where someone lit special candles for Sabbaths or holidays, did you ever witness a moment of warmth and significance when you visited a friend or relative who closed their eyes, said something from the heart, and lit a flame that had some intrigue and dancing colors emerging from its glow?

This chapter is not about the rules or logistics of lighting candles. (There are many other places on the internet or from books, articles, or teachers where you can find detailed discussions of how to light holy candles).

Rather, this chapter is about some of the deeper meanings and creative inspirations that many Jews experience as a result of lighting candles or opening up to the light of those candles. Whether you are religious, not-very-religious, or not-at-all-religious, you are invited to explore in the next several pages what happens to our inner light and to the light we bring into this fragile world when we take a moment out of our busy lives and we light a flame that dances in front of our eyes and deep within our hearts.

Specifically, this chapter will focus on four different ways that lighting a candle and saying a blessing over those lights can stir up beneficial outcomes for you and your loved ones. Please take a quick glimpse at these four different creative possibilities and see if one or more of them might be enjoyable for you to explore further on your own:

Increasing the Light #1: Discovering That You Can Shift Your Central Nervous System from a Feeling of Agitation to a Feeling of Being Renewed and Refreshed

Each of us human beings have certain sensory moments when our nerves and our thoughts can suddenly shift out of being anxious and instead open up to a feeling of calmness. For instance, I have a friend who has been meditating for many years and each time he hears the sound of the wood mallet striking the bronze bowl he feels his nerve endings relaxing and his mind entering a more centered, calm state. Another friend of mine is a woman who loves the smell and the taste of home-brewed coffee and she describes how her body relaxes and her mind feels less agitated when she senses the aroma of the delicious coffee she is about to taste.

Yet another friend is someone who grew up in Southern California and remembers the feeling that she and her brother experienced each time as kids when they were in the back seat being driven by their parents to Disneyland and as soon as they saw in the distance from the freeway the sight of the Matterhorn ride, they both felt extremely happy and excited because they were about to enter "their happy place."

I grew up in Michigan having a somewhat similar feeling of joy and hopeful anticipation when my parents or an older friend would drive me out of the city to spend several hours at Kensington Park where we could swim in the lake and picnic along the shore. That sensory feeling of sweet delight would come over me as soon as I saw the clusters of trees and the expansive blue water in the distance.

These visceral moments of feeling your body and mind shifting from the stresses of daily life and going instead to a place of deep relaxation and enjoyment are very similar to what millions of Jewish individuals and families have experienced for many, many centuries when they stepped out of "high-pressure time" and entered a world of "gentle, relaxed, connecting time" at the moment when they lit (or someone else lit) the Sabbath candles on Friday night. Maybe you have had that experience one or more times in your life—when after a very intense and difficult week, you looked at the glowing Sabbath candles and you felt a sense of letting go and shifting into a much more relaxed and pleasurable frame of mind. Or maybe it's not something you have experienced personally, but you have heard from others that there is a remarkable moment possible when taking a nurturing breath, lighting the candles, and saying a blessing from the heart can suddenly cause the nerve endings, the tense muscles, and the agitated brain to calm down significantly.

As a child, I didn't fully understand what the Sabbath or the lighting of candles were about. But starting in my 20's I frequently attended a Friday night service where the rabbi at that congregation did something each week immediately before the Friday night candle lighting that I still remember vividly because of how it transformed my over-worked nervous system and my racing thoughts. This compassionate rabbi, who had an extensive background in Jewish meditation and Kabbalah, would take a deep breath in and out at the beginning of the Friday night gatherings—a long, relaxing inhale followed by a long, relaxing exhale.

Then the rabbi would ask the congregation to take a similar long gentle inhale followed by a long gentle exhale. With a comforting sigh that came from deep inside, the rabbi would then say slowly, "Oy. I don't know what kind of week you had. But this was an intense week for me and my family. I'm very relieved that it's finally Shabbat. So, whatever you did or didn't accomplish or finish this week, right now it's a moment to say to yourself, 'You did a lot. You did plenty. You can gently let go of the thoughts that are saying you should have done more. Right now, you are enough. You are more than enough. You can breathe and know that right at this moment we can take the pressure off for twenty-four hours. It's Shabbat. Shabbat Shalom."

Then someone from the congregation would say the blessing and light the Sabbath candles. At that quiet moment, most of us in the congregation would breathe in and out gently in the silence and you could feel the energy shifting in the room. Suddenly we were no longer a bunch of busy, striving humans who had rushed to get to services on time. Suddenly we were in a transformative moment where the stress of the week would (to a great extent) be untangled and softened by hearing the rabbi's words and seeing the candle flames dancing in front of us.

Instead of our adrenal glands being overloaded like we all were a few minutes earlier, now we were starting to sing together a beautiful melody as we welcomed in the Sabbath. That feeling of shifting out of "stress time" and shifting into "Sabbath time" has stayed with me and I recall it often when I am at home and the candles are lit or I am at a Friday night service and I see the congregation breathing, relaxing, and singing in front of the dancing glow of the lit candles.

Is it possible for someone who didn't grow up with Sabbath candles to experience that kind of relaxing sensory shift? I've found that many people who are lighting candles at home for the first time, or being part of a Friday night service with a congregation for the first time, get more and more of the calmness each time they do it (and less and less of the insecure thoughts of "Am I doing it right.") Usually after two or more times of enjoying the lit candles you begin to realize, "Wow. I was tense and rushing a few minutes ago. But right now, I am fully present and feeling a lot more peaceful."

Are you interested in the possibility that your own body and mind will feel more relaxed and calm the next time you participate in a Friday night candle-lighting or a holiday dinner where the candles are glowing? I can't guarantee this feeling of peacefulness will happen for you each and every time you light candles and enter into Sabbath mode. But based on the hundreds of people I have talked with personally who have made Sabbath candles and blessings a joyful part of their life during their teens, 20's, 30's, 40's, or later, I would estimate that more than 75% of the time when someone takes a quiet moment to close their eyes, breathe calmly, envision the light within us and the light surrounding us, and then say a blessing from the heart as you strike a match and touch it to the candle wicks, you will be amazed at how it can noticeably shift your energy and free you from being enslaved by the pressures of your life.

The words that you can say when you bless the holy lights of the Sabbath or a holiday are:

Bah-rookh Ahtah Adonai (or HaShem the mysterious Name of the One who is beyond human words),

Eloheinu Melekh Ha-Olahm,

Ahshayr Keed-shahnu B'mitz-vo-tahv,

V'tzee-vah-nu, L'Hahdleek Nayr (Shel Shabbat or Shel Yom Tov)

Which can be translated as: Blessed are You, Eternal One, the ongoing Source that was, that is, and that will be, our God Who guides the universe, Who blesses us with mitzvot (good deeds, commandments) and Who guides (or) commands us to light the lights (of Sabbath or of a holiday).

Or another version might be: "Thank You, Eternal Source, for guiding us to light these holy lights."

As you say it slowly, let yourself envision a flow of energy transmitting some of your inner light to the light of the candles and then, in turn, seeing how the light of the candles moves in your direction (and to the others in the room) and adds to each of your inner lights.

Increasing the Light #2: Discovering That You Can Connect with the Sacred Jewish Priestess Tradition That is Re-emerging Today

If you ask most people, "Who comes to mind as the person who is lighting the Sabbath candles," many of them will talk about their grandmothers or the housewife in "Fiddler on the Roof" who covered her eyes, lit the candles, and sang the beautiful song "Hear Our Sabbath Prayer" in the stage version or the movie version.

Rarely does someone think of the more modern examples of Shabbat candle lighting that we now see all over the world, including:

- The twelve-year-old or thirteen-year-old who is lighting Shabbat candles for the first time and rising up to help lead the family in a holy moment of being together.

- The high school students at Shabbat youth group events all over the world who are getting crushes on each other and feeling a sense of closeness when they are together for a Sabbath gathering that consists of their peers and friends.

- The Hillel students at hundreds of colleges and universities who cover their eyes, sing the blessing, and help all the guests and visitors feel connected on a campus (where they may have felt sometimes like outsiders prior to that connecting moment of watching the glow of the candles together with people who might then become profound friends, sometimes for the rest of their lives after meeting at an informal Shabbat event).

- The young adults who invite a few friends over on Friday night and they light candles as part of an enjoyable evening of deep conversations, laughter, good food, and music that is a welcome contrast to the high-pressure world of work and status.

- The families all over the world who barely see each other during the week because of their busy schedules, but on Friday night they are together with their arms around each other watching the Shabbat candles.

- The people of all ages who are single and dating someone relatively new who comes over for a Friday night dinner and as the candles are lit, they feel a little closer (and the Shabbat dinner at someone's home has an extra sense of depth and openness than just going out to a busy, noisy restaurant).

- The elders lighting candles on well-worn, old-school candle holders that they've used for decades and feeling a wave of beautiful memories of Shabbat dinners in the past. There is something so holy and profound about someone in their 60's, 70's, 80's, or 90's saying the prayer over the candles with deep sincerity (even if they have said it many hundreds of times before).

In addition, there is a spiritual aspect to the lighting of candles that most Jews today never learned about during their many years of Jewish education, but that is very much alive and growing in several parts of the world right now. I am talking about the Jewish Priestess Tradition that existed in ancient times, got de-emphasized for many centuries, and is now making a comeback. Here's what I mean by "The Jewish Priestess Tradition:"

Eleven years ago, I attended a weeklong workshop that dealt with "New and Old Forms of Feminist Jewish Spirituality." One of the classes I participated in was taught by a prolific woman writer and counselor named Nina Amir, who has written eBooks and articles about how the lighting of the Sabbath candles is a continuation of the "Creating a Beautiful Sacred Space" leadership of Hebrew Priestesses in ancient, medieval and modern Judaism.

According to Nina Amir and several other authors and scholars who have written about this rarely-discussed aspect of Jewish tradition, the importance of the Hebrew Priestess goes back to Miriam the Prophetess, Deborah the Judge and Leader, and many other unnamed

Jewish female leaders in the Torah (and this Hebrew Priestess tradition continues to this day). Part of the leadership responsibilities of the Jewish Priestess has been to preside over holy spaces for various Jewish rituals, including the Friday night details that include:

- Making the ordinary, everyday table in your kitchen, or dining room, or in the social hall at the temple or synagogue, into a sacred altar space.

- Bringing in natural elements such as flowers, herbs, wine, water, beautiful fabrics, and inspiring colorful patterns.

- Putting on a beautiful shawl or head covering (and other special clothes) that help you feel in charge of the ritual.

- Then saying the ancient words and moving your hands in such a way that you are able to transform the energy in the room to raise up the consciousness of everyone present.

The Hebrew Priestess was not just a "dutiful wife" or "help mate," but rather a true leader, a spiritual channel for divine energies, and a wise teacher of sacred information and holy methods. Even if your grandmother would roll her eyes and say, "Feh, I'm just lighting the candles the way my mother lit the candles. It's just something I do to keep the tradition," in fact she was also participating in a more ancient tradition of being a Hebrew Priestess who feels the energy, raises up the energy, and moves the energy toward each of the complicated individuals gathered in the room.

Is this tradition of the Hebrew Priestess something that you have been taught in any of your Jewish education (or was it left out for some reason)? Is the leadership role of being the person who can channel holy energies, create sacred spaces, and lead important rituals something that you have explored in your own life or in any of the Rosh Hodesh (monthly new moon gatherings) that have become increasingly attended in recent years in many congregations?

I realized after studying with Nina Amir in 2011 that this crucial information about the importance of the Hebrew Priestess tradition had been left out of my Jewish education and that it was up to me to make sure I explored it more. Then in 2015, I read a thought-provoking book called "The Hebrew Priestess: Ancient and New Visions of Jewish Women's Spiritual Leadership" by Rabbi Jill Hammer and Taya Shere, who are the co-founders of the Kohenet Hebrew Priestess Institute. I learned a tremendous amount about how Judaism has always been connected to Mother Earth and to the healing wisdom and transformative powers of female spiritual leaders.

I also began to experience with new eyes the Friday night candle lighting (as well as the candles lit at Havdalah on Saturday nights and at various holidays either at home or in a synagogue or temple). Now when I see someone (whether it is a woman or a man or a non-binary individual) covering their eyes, breathing calmly, waving their hands in small circles to transmit energy, and saying blessings from the heart over the candles, I feel as if I am witnessing a profound Jewish tradition of gifted Priestesses who are taking us into this new century with greater wisdom about saving the planet, healing what is broken in our world, and connecting us with a more expansive sense of sacred beauty and sacred ritual.

Here's how you or a loved one can experiment with seeing the candle-lighting on a Friday night or a holiday as a sacred moment with a strong connection to the Hebrew Priestess tradition:

- Look at the table, podium or countertop where the candle holders and candles will be lit. Envision that it is not just a table, a podium, or a countertop, but rather it is becoming (with your creative ideas and unique style) a sacred altar for an ancient and transformative ceremony.

- Decide on what beautiful fabric, what inspiring patterns and colors, what flowers or herbs, what special plates, special glasses, special silverware, special napkins you would like to add to this ceremony in order to raise up its holiness and its power to take you and the other participants to a sacred space and an expanded awareness that is not just an ordinary, mundane moment.

- As you prepare to say the blessing and light the candles, envision yourself as being part of a Hebrew Priestess tradition that has been transmitting wisdom and healing energies for numerous centuries. Not only are there Hebrew Priestesses all over the world today saying these prayers in small and large venues to connect with the subtle and mysterious energies of the Sabbath or a holiday. But there have been wise and powerful Priestesses saying these same prayers and transforming the energy throughout all ages.

- Then as you say the blessings, light the candles, and wave your hands in small circles to spread the light to each of those who are gathered, take a moment to sense how the energy is moving in the room. You might envision as you wave your hands in small circles that the love and strength that is in your heart is actually spreading to each of the people in the room and, in turn, coming back to you to add to your own love and strength. You are not someone just going through the motions of a rigid custom by lighting these lights. Instead, you are engaged in a visually beautiful, timeless, sacred moment of boosting the energy for each beloved soul gathered around these glowing lights.

Increasing the Light #3: If You Would Like, You Can Create a Dress Rehearsal for a Time of Peace and Cooperation.

Now we are switching perspectives for a moment to one additional fascinating teaching about Shabbat candles and Shabbat experiences. If you study the Kabbalistic interpretations of the glowing candles and the Sabbath, you will find they are sometimes described as an outline or a practice session for creating a tactile preview of what life could be like if we ever reach the level of harmony, peace, equality, and sufficiency in the world. According to the Kabbalists and many other Jewish scholars, the Sabbath is a day of envisioning what our world might be like if there were no hunger or shortages. It's asking us to explore what would life be like if there were no prejudices or discrimination against those who are different from the majority. It's encouraging us to discover what would life be like if people didn't have to compete for scarce resources but rather there was sufficient distribution and care for the Earth so that everyone could have enough.

What a fascinating concept! In the dancing light of the Shabbat candles, we are being asked to take a breath and imagine what life on Earth would be like if we stopped mistreating one another and if we set up sensible systems to make sure everyone had enough and didn't have to suffer from shortages, corruption, or greed.

What you might not have been taught in your Jewish education is that the Kabbalah and many other Jewish sources have described the Sabbath as a practice session (or a dress rehearsal), a day to experience with your own actions what that time of peace and cooperation would look like and feel like. That's why on the Sabbath you don't have to work or strive, because you are envisioning for several hours (or for an entire 24 hours), what it would be like to celebrate at meals with loved ones and guests where there was more than enough for everyone. That's why on the Sabbath, many people enact what it would feel like if we were absolutely free to take walks, dance, sing, read inspiring books, have deep conversations, take a nap, make love, unhook from some of our electronic gadgets, and stay away from anything that drains your energy or diminishes your soul. Some have called it a day for practicing what "heaven on Earth" would feel like.

If you grew up thinking that the Jewish Sabbath was simply a bunch of harsh restrictions and things you are not allowed to do, please take a moment to rethink that short-sighted view (for your own life from now on or for your loved ones as well). You now have a new chance to decide what you want to do (and what you don't want to do) on an upcoming Sabbath based on what the Kabbalah and many other Jewish sources would suggest—that this might be a good time to let go of (for a few hours or for an entire 24 hours) the striving, the pressure, the competing, the comparing, the regretting, the agitating. For a few hours or for 24 hours, what if you envisioned and did a practice session on what would be nourishing and enjoyable if the world were at peace, if you didn't have to struggle or compete in order to have enough, and if you could spend quality time with the people, ideas, music, nature, and restful intimate moments you often can't do during the busy work week.

Here's a very practical way to experience the candle-lighting and the Sabbath not as a bunch of restrictions, but rather as a series of "spiritual gift certificates" for a "Day of Peace and Warmth." Please check into your own heart to see if you want to bring some of these ideas into your own life for the Sabbaths that you and your loved ones can enjoy in the next few weeks, months, or years:

- Imagine for a moment that someone who cares about you has sent you a gift certificate for a day that is to be devoted entirely to the needs of your soul.

- On that day (set apart from the other six days), you don't have to work or pressure yourself to get a lot of trivial things done.

- You can take a walk and have a relaxing, unrushed conversation with friends or loved ones about the things that really matter.

- You can meditate, pray, sing, connect with a spiritual community that uplifts your spirit, and read the books that speak to your soul.

- You can nap and let your mind take a rest, or dance and sing to let your spirit soar.

- For one day, you can stop trying to prove yourself out in the world.

- You can look at your life as a blessing and feel at peace with how much you are learning each week.

- Instead of feeling fragmented and pressured, you can spend the day in a generous, positive, and contemplative mood.

Are you interested in exploring personally what it would feel like to have a half day or an entire day of enjoying some of these Sabbath gift cards that are available to you right now? As a first step, ask yourself calmly, "Is there one thing I would like to add to my Sabbath next weekend so that it feels more like a day that nurtures my soul?" and "Is there one thing I would like to stop doing on the Sabbath so that I don't feel drained or pulled away from what is most nourishing for my soul?" If you follow through on just those two visions for "a day that is a dress rehearsal for a time of peace and sufficiency," your body, your mind, and your soul will feel more refreshed and renewed for dealing with all the challenges that will come up during the week that follows.

Increasing the Light #4: Rather Than Feeling Isolated, You Can Create Your Own Circle of Interesting People and Connecting Moments

One of the most uplifting parts of lighting candles and being part of a Sabbath ceremony at your home, or at someone else's home, or in a warm, welcoming congregation, is that it gives us a chance to stop being so isolated and instead to build new connections to people who are inspiring, caring, and thoughtful. If you have ever felt isolated in a fast-paced city, or alone after the breakup of a relationship or the loss of a loved one, or like "a fish out of water" because your unique interests are somewhat different from the majority of people you work with or live near, then the chance to light candles and sing together with some decent people who are smart, caring, and creative becomes even more important and nourishing.

Are you interested in feeling less isolated and more a part of something holy? Sometimes we get depleted or knocked off center by the pressures and difficulties of the week, yet if we can find a supportive circle of good souls for a Friday night candle-lighting, meal, and deep discussions, it can significantly restore our energy. If we can connect each week or each month with a congregation of compassionate and creative individuals who truly care about one another (and are welcoming to you and your loved ones), then we are no longer "strangers in a strange land."

Here are a few ideas of how to overcome the isolation or alienation so many people are feeling these days, and instead create a circle of allies and caring faces for a Friday night candle-lighting moment or a Shabbat gathering that boosts up your ability to deal with all that life has been tossing at you lately. Please note which of the following you are already doing to raise up your energy and which of these ideas might be useful for future Shabbats for you and your loved ones:

- Instead of waiting for someone else to make the first move, go ahead and invite one or two or seven people that you care about, or enjoy being with, to your home for a Friday night candle-lighting that gives each of you a sense of, "Wow, that was an intense week. But right now, we are unhooking from the rat race for a moment and we're enjoying being together."

- Show up weekly or monthly at a congregation where you like the way they welcome you and your loved ones, where you enjoy the way they bring in the Sabbath, where the melodies and teachings nourish your soul, and where you feel that your uniqueness is respected and appreciated.

- Create a Shabbat dinner group or holiday group that meets once a month or a few times a year and allows each participant the chance to bring one of their favorite food items for a joyous potluck meal (with an email or text ahead of time that helps people be respectful of the food guidelines or other dietary issues that will make the gathering comfortable for everyone who will be there).

- Start a tradition in your congregation where once a month or a few times a year, several members of the congregation act as hosts to invite to their homes (on a Friday night for Shabbat candles or a Saturday night for Havdalah candles) some smaller gatherings of current members, new members, and guests for an evening where everyone has a chance to share stories and get to know one another better.

- You can also have these gatherings around a particular theme. For instance, once a month or a few times a year, there can be an evening where everyone is invited to bring a favorite piece of music (and the three-minute back-story of why that piece of music means so much to you), or a favorite charity (and a three-minute description of why that charity inspires you and why you want others to know about it), or a favorite quick story about your roots or your ancestors, or an evening where each of you brings a favorite religious or household object that you were given by a loved one (and a three-minute description of why that particular object has so much meaning and importance).

- Encourage your congregation to have some special themes that add to the light and the depth of the Shabbat gatherings. One possibility is to have a few minutes during Sabbath services or meals at home where everyone has a chance to think about a very personal and relevant topic that comes from that week's Torah portion.

For example, at our congregation for the past few years, we have notified everyone in the weekly newsletter what the personalized Torah-based theme of the week is for all of us to think about as Shabbat approaches and then in the middle of services a few volunteers give a brief, two-minute, intimate story about that personal theme, such as:

On the week that Jacob and Esau are clashing, the theme in the newsletter that everyone is encouraged to think about (and that a few volunteers then share their personal stories about in the middle of services) is "What were the tense moments with a sibling of yours and how has that relationship improved or not improved over the years." I remember how each person in the congregation was moved and paying close attention as we listened to a few two-minute descriptions of how fellow congregants tried to heal their tensions with a sibling. It made the Torah portion and the entire service extremely alive and timely for each of us.

Or on the week that Abraham and Sarah change their names and begin to go out "to a place they did not know," the theme that was described in the newsletter and discussed at services was, "When in your life did you take a leap of faith and go forward even though you were somewhat afraid?" Whether a congregant was a teenager, a young adult, a mid-life adult, or a senior, we all could relate to the three volunteers at services giving two-minute descriptions of how they dealt with the fears that hold us back and how they journeyed forward "to a place they did not know."

Or on the week that Miriam leads the Hebrews in song and dance after the parting of the waters, the theme for discussion was, "What are the moments in your life when you were so overjoyed and grateful that you felt like singing or dancing?" That brief discussion in our congregation caused each person in the room to think about the joyous moments they have celebrated and to start planning creative ways to celebrate the joyous moments that might be coming up in the next few months or years.

Or on the week that Sarah finds out that Abraham almost sacrificed their beloved son Isaac, the theme was, "Have you ever felt left out of an important decision and what have you learned about making sure you get included and not silenced?" As I looked around the room at the many faces of those who were at services that week, I could see this quick discussion of "how to make sure your voice and your input doesn't get left out" was an important theme for almost everyone there.

When a Shabbat dinner, or a Shabbat service, or any holiday during the year has a brief, inspiring conversation topic that everyone can relate to from their own lives, we not only learn from one another, but we also feel a stronger sense of connection to each other. Suddenly these are not just strangers or isolated individuals around you, but rather they are deeply insightful and caring people that you want to get to know better because you have discussed important topics together in a caring way.

When I have traveled around the country, I've noticed that in some congregations they give each and every individual a chance to speak for two or three minutes about the theme of the week by having every person in the congregation turn to the person next to them and (with one person going first and the other person speaking after two minutes) they briefly answer the question of, "What is a moment in your life when you experienced what is in this week's Torah portion: sibling rivalry; taking a leap of faith and making a new start; celebrating with dance or song; making sure you aren't left out of important decisions, etc." It not only highlights that week's Torah teachings, but it causes people to feel more involved and more connected as a caring community at each weekly prayer service. Having the chance to open up your heart and be honest in a quick, profound conversation with the person next to you is a powerful way to break out of isolation and feel fully alive as we search together for moments of holiness and healing.

Once again, I am hoping that if you were raised with very little or no connection to the beauty and visionary aspects of Shabbat candle-lighting, holiday dinners, and Sabbath services (or if you were raised with a lot of harsh restrictions and not much of the joy), these somewhat different ideas and possibilities might open new chances for you to create meaningful connections and uplifting moments each time you are lighting candles or participating in a Shabbat or holiday gathering.

There are an endless number of possibilities and the list above is just to get you started. Please feel free to come up with your own ideas or brainstorm with your loved ones, friends, and congregation members to make sure that each week you find a way to unhook from the external pressures and tap into an endless flow of Shabbat light and renewal that will nourish your soul. Whether you are 12, or 22, or 52, or 82, your next several Sabbaths and candle lighting experiences could become moments when you feel your body relaxing and where you connect with some new insights for dealing with what really matters in life.

CHAPTER EIGHT:

What Makes Each Meal More Meaningful?

In this final chapter, we're going to be talking about food. You might want to bring a snack or read some of these pages at the table where you are having a delicious meal. You will be amazed at how much of a connection there is between how we live spiritually and how we relate to food and nourishment.

For an appetizer, I'd like to start with a true story: When I was fifteen years old and at my very first youth group retreat weekend at an old, log-cabin lodge in the woods in Michigan (with high school students from my congregation and from several other congregations), we did an exercise that I have never forgotten.

At the Sunday lunch on that retreat weekend, everyone was instructed to tie a fourteen-inch wood stick to each of their arms (from the bicep muscle in the upper arm to the wrist in the lower arm) so that you couldn't bend your arm at the elbow and therefore you couldn't bring your hand up to your mouth to feed yourself. We quickly discovered that the only way to eat at that lunch is if you used your outstretched arm to feed the person across from you and then that person fed you with their outstretched arm.

The meal was slow, sometimes humorous, and quite thought-pro-voking. Every small fork-full of food was carefully choreographed to reach the mouth of the person across from you without spilling too much. Each person felt extremely focused, very present, and defi-nitely dependent and reliant on one another. It was a meal in which you noticed and felt grateful for even the smallest, delicious bite of food that reached your lips and soothed your hunger. The simple act of having a meal was suddenly more meaningful than if we had just rushed through it.

In Judaism, there are some brilliant and nourishing words that can be said at the start of every meal to slow us down from gulping our food and to raise us up to notice the important sources of what we are enjoying. These very brief prayer phrases also connect us with the beauty of being alive and being nourished. Even if you have said a few of these words many times in your life, I hope you will discover new information and new possibilities as you read these next several pages.

Here are three different ways for connecting with the extra burst of aliveness that can come from the specific words you say when you sit down to enjoy a snack or a meal:

Deepened Experience #1: How to Boost Your Awareness of the Important Ingredients

If you ask a five, or a seven, or a ten-year old kid if they read carefully the ingredients section on the packaging of food that they are going to be eating, most kids will look at you with a skeptical face and say, "Are you kidding? Why would I want to do that?"

But at a certain age, most of us begin to notice and to become aware that some foods have ingredients that make you feel alert and focused, while other foods have ingredients that tend to give you (or someone you are cooking for) some mild or not-so-mild digestive issues, or these particular ingredients tend to make you feel sleepy, un-focused, or a little bit hyper.

What about you and the people in your life right now? Do you (or your loved ones or roommates) have any food allergies or food sensitivities that you now watch for as you consider the ingredients? Are there any specific foods or additives that you try to avoid when you are shopping at a store, choosing from a restaurant menu with your health in mind, or when you are managing your intake of salt, or sugar, or fats, or specific ingredients that give you trouble, or when you are making sure you get enough protein, fiber, vitamins, and minerals that keep your body and mind functioning well?

In Judaism for many centuries, there has been a beautiful and mindful moment that you can do (on your own or with the people around you) when you sit down for a snack or a meal. Instead of rushing in and mindlessly gobbling down the food without any awareness of what's going into your body, there is a quite-useful tradition in Judaism to slow down for a moment and ask yourself, "What is in front of me right now?" Very quickly you take note of what's in the food you are about to eat, and you consciously decide which of several prayer phrases to say for this particular nourishing treat.

This quick, relaxing moment before starting to eat not only helps you avoid foods that cause trouble, but it also opens up your awareness to the fact that this food has a fascinating back-story which includes sunlight from a mysterious Source, plus rain, soil, winds, careful farming, a vast distribution network, and some artful cooks who brought this delicious food item from farm to table. Suddenly you are not just chomping down a meaningless nothing, but rather you are connecting with the Creative Life Force, the Breath of the Universe, and how it generously provides us with nourishment through a series of steps and processes that are quite fascinating if you take a moment to consider them.

Here are the choices of a few, very quick, Hebrew and English prayer phrases that you can select from in order to boost your awareness of what you are about to take into your body as nourishment:

If it's bread you are about to eat, then you might say the very familiar prayer phrase that most Jews of all ages know by heart:

Bah-rookh Ahtah Adonai (or HaShem, the mysterious name of the One that is beyond names)

Eloheinu melekh ha-olam

Ha-motzi lekhem min ha-ahretz.

Blessed are You, Eternal Source, our God who guides the universe, Who brings forth bread from the Earth.

Or if you are about to eat something that is a fruit from a tree, you might say:

Bah-rookh Ahtah Adonai (or HaShem)

Eloheinu melekh ha-olam

Bo-rei p'ri ha-eitz.

Blessed are You, Eternal Source, our God who guides the universe, Who creates the fruit of the tree.

Or if it is grape wine or grape juice, you might say:

Bah-rookh Ahtah Adonai (or HaShem)

Eloheinu melekh ha-olam

Bo-rei p'ri ha-gahfen.

Blessed are You, Eternal Source, our God who guides the universe, Who creates the fruit of the vine.

Or if you are about to eat something that grows directly from the Earth (like a vegetable, or a root plant, or a legume, or a mushroom), you might say:

Bah-rookh Ahtah Adonai (or HaShem)

Eloheinu melekh ha-olam

Bo-rei p'ri ha-adahmah.

Blessed are You, Eternal Source, our God who guides the universe,

Who creates the fruits of the ground.

Or if you are about to eat something that is a combination of grains such as wheat, barley, rye, oats, spelt, or (according to many opinions) rice, then you might say:

Bah-rookh Ahtah Adonai (or HaShem)

Eloheinu melekh ha-olam

Bo-rei mih-nei m'zohnoht.

Blessed are You, Eternal Source, our God who guides the universe,

Who creates species of nourishment.

Or if it is a diverse combination of several different types of food or ingredients, you might say:

Bah-rookh Ahtah Adonai (or HaShem)

Eloheinu melekh ha-olam

Sheh-hakol nih-hih-yeh bid-varo.

Blessed are You, Eternal Source, our God who guides the universe,

through Whose Expressing everything came to be.

At that moment of slowing down and being mindful of what is in front of you, you can envision a Creative Life Force infusing the world with sunlight, nutrition for the soil, rain for growing crops, enormously diverse choices, and the wisdom of those who tend the crops, bring the nutritious foods to market, and prepare the foods lovingly. Suddenly it's not just your fork feeding your mouth, but it's your entire soul being deeply aware of the nourishing, connected Web of Life that we can tap into with each bite of food.

The next time you sit down for a nourishing breakfast, lunch, dinner, or snack, see if you can experience any or all of these extra benefits from having said a prayer:

- You might experience a moment of clarity that today you are ready to start saying no to some of the ingredients that tend to drain your energy, or that make you feel sleepy, edgy, or impatient a few minutes after eating them.

- You might experience a moment of clarity that you are not alone in the world, but rather you are nourished by all sorts of people and natural settings near and far that helped grow, pick, or prepare this delicious food (and that you might not see with your own eyes but that you can thank from your heart). Just like the experience I had at age fifteen when each person at the table realized we are absolutely reliant on one another in order to eat, the Hebrew and English words you say (silently or quietly) might connect you with the realization that there are people, natural processes, and a mysterious Creative Source of sunlight, wind, rain, and agricultural wisdom that helped this food arrive onto the plate in front of you.

- You might experience a sensory moment of clarity when as a result of slowing down to say a quick prayer, you find that you are able to notice more than usual the exquisite taste, the delicate texture, the comforting feeling, and the nutritious elements of what you are bringing to your lips. Instead of devouring the food with no consciousness of how delicious it is, the act of saying a few holy words before eating can cause you to have a much more sensual and enjoyable experience of appreciating each bite or sip.

In other words, for many centuries Jews have had the opportunity to take a breath, increase their awareness of what the snack or meal contains, and be more present, thankful, and less "out to lunch" in the way we take nourishment into our bodies. The prayer phrase that you possibly thought as a teenager was just a rigid ob-ligation from some authority figure, or an irritating speed bump to rush through, becomes far more interesting and useful when you see it as a moment of mindfulness and profound gratitude for what you are about to eat.

Please note: I am not saying you have to obsess before every snack or meal and find the exact 100% correct version of the prayer for the precise, specific ingredients in front of you each and every time you eat. The diverse prayer-phrase-choices are written out for you if you might want them, but in reality most Jews take a breath, stop for a quick moment to consider the ingredients of what they are about to eat, and then say one particular favorite "go-to phrase" at most meals and snacks.

Some choose to say at most meals "ha-motzi lekhem min ha-ahretz" (and translate it is as "Who brings forth food from the Earth") as the go-to standard phrase they connect with in a mindful way before every meal or snack. Some use "sheh-hakol nih-hih-yeh bid-va-ro" (and translate it as "Thank you to the One who expresses and everything comes to be") as the most reliable phrase they say during a peaceful moment before eating. Some tend to select "bo-rei mih-nei m'zohnoht" (and translate it as "Thank you, Eternal Source, for creating each of these different types of nourishment") as the most frequent prayer they say when they are about to eat a meal that has several ingredients.

The goal is not to obsess or be bogged down by the details, but rather to give yourself a quick moment of increased awareness and calmness. I invite you to select which of the options mentioned ear-lier is your own favorite choice, that inspires you the most for being grateful and aware of the miracle of being nourished and being alive. On some days you might choose to pick the exact correct phrase, while on other days you might choose to go with your own favorite standard phrase that encompasses all the other phrases.

Or on other days, you might say your own words of gratitude and centering in your own spontaneous way. In fact, many people find during the quick prayer they say in their own creative, original words before a meal that those relaxed moments of spontaneous appreciation for even one small thing, plus slowing down for a few seconds for feeling thankful, make a huge difference in whether life feels like an exhausting race or whether it feels sane and holy.

The Man Who Definitely Didn't Like Praying Before a Meal

Not everyone is comfortable saying a prayer at breakfast, lunch, or dinner. If you were raised in a family where before each meal there was anger and rigid rules that sounded like, "Now shut your mouth, bow your head, and say your prayers, you little brat," you might have a bit of hesitation or resistance about this process of stopping before a meal and saying something mindful and spiritual.

For example, one of my friends is a movie producer with an amazing sense of humor and insight. He loves to tell jokes and find the absurd irony in almost everything. Part of his quick sense of humor comes from his tense upbringing and how he survived his very controlling parents and older siblings. He grew up in a family where his parents were frequently yelling at the kids and shaming them for not doing exactly what the parents wanted.

So when this friend and I were at lunch one day and I took a moment to breathe and say a quick, softly-spoken prayer before digging into the food, my friend laughed dismissively and said playfully, "Oh, I hate when people get all spiritual on me and stop to say their prayers and they let the food get cold. I feel like writing a note afterward to the chef and saying, 'I apologize that we took that extra few seconds to start eating. If we had just skipped the prayer, we could have appreciated your amazing creation at its perfect temperature."

I've known this guy for many years and I've seen him be snarky at times, but I've also seen him be vulnerable, empathic, and quite philosophical many times. As we began to take a first few bites of the delicious food, I gently said, "I noticed that my saying a prayer caused you to flash back on the harsh rules that you had to put up with as a kid. I'm sorry about that."

He smiled and said, "Not to worry. I don't live by those rules anymore. When I was seventeen and my dad screamed in my face, 'As long as you are under MY ROOF you will do things MY WAY,' I packed up my stuff and I decided to go find a new roof. Best decision I ever made."

I smiled and commented, "Yep. You've come a long way since then. But can I ask you a question?"

He replied, "Sure. What can I enlighten you about today?"

I spoke carefully and said, "We've known each other for many years and I appreciate that spirituality is not your cup of tea. At the same time, it's pretty interesting that what you just said about acknowledging the chef and the amazing creative process that caused this carefully-prepared food to be in front of us right now is exactly the reason why most people say a quick prayer before eating. It's not about being compliant to a rigid parent who insisted, 'hurry up and say your prayers,' but more about appreciating the back-story, the ingredients, the creative process, the producers, the crew, the teamwork, maybe even the bank employee who arranged the loan for this entrepreneurial chef to start his own place, and everything else that led to this moment of enjoying this delicious food. When your heart opened up just now to a sense of appreciation and awe about the creative chef and this beautiful creation, you were doing what the prayer is intended to do—you were being appreciative that we're grateful for the amazing process and creative sources that brought us this excellent meal."

My friend looked at me and said, "Nice try Mr. Spiritual Dude, but when I grew up with my controlling dad and we would say 'Rub a dub dub, thanks for the grub, yay God,' it wasn't about being mindful or appreciative. It was just us kids being silly and sassy."

I replied, "Okay, I agree that sometimes a kid just says something because it's fun or provocative to say. But that was then and yet right now you are a tough, no-nonsense film guy who has an appreciation for how much energy and teamwork goes into making a film or any creative project, and you were able to feel grateful to the creative chef and all the talent, persistence, care, and unknowable mystery that went into this food. After what you experienced as a kid in your family, it makes perfect sense that you don't like the word 'spiritual' but let's face it—you happen to be someone who is able to see beyond the surface layer and be aware of the behind-the-scenes process that can make beautiful things happen. That's what a prayer or a spiritual awareness is about. Even though you don't like the word, you my friend are 'spiritual' in the best sense of the word because you're able to look at something mundane and everyday—like a plate of food—and yet somehow you can connect with the fact that this food has so many caring and generous creative steps and sources that we can appreciate if we stop for a moment to raise up our awareness."

My friend nodded his head a little as he was chewing his food and he replied, "Okay, maybe I did mention that the creative chef needs to be given some credit and that I'm grateful and aware of the amazing process. Maybe that's one definition of being spiritual."

Then he smiled and said, "But if being aware and appreciative for what goes on behind the scenes makes me 'spiritual,' then just don't tell my wife and my kids that I said something grateful and sensitive at lunch today. They might think I'm going soft after all these years."

I nodded my head in agreement. I said, "I promise I won't tell them just how mindful and thankful you are, or that you have a deep sense of awe for life and creativity. I promise I won't ruin your cover." He smiled. I smiled. Then we went back to enjoying the meal.

What about you? Would you be uncomfortable or embarrassed if someone noticed that you were stopping for a few seconds before a meal to explore what are the specific ingredients and what is the awesome creative process that brought this meal to the table in front of you? Like my longtime friend the movie producer, would you be worried that to have a quick thoughtful pause before eating a meal might make you "a little too out there" or a "little too spiritual?" If so, you have the option of not closing your eyes and not moving your lips. You can take a quick moment to appreciate the ingredients and the Source of the food you are eating by letting these thoughts of gratitude come up from your heart and into your brain without ever letting anyone else in the room know that you are praying. The choice is yours on whether to pray openly or very secretly. Either way, you will have given yourself a moment to feel calm, centered, and grateful before the first morsels of food reach your lips.

Deepened Experience #2: Learning How to Treat Your Body as a "Holy Vessel."

Is it possible that preparing food and enjoying food can be a holy experience? One of the things I love about Judaism is how much kindness and respect we are taught to have for the human body. Every day we are encouraged to say a prayer of thanks that our fragile and complicated body works as well as it does. When a person dies, the body is gently washed and cared for with deep love and respect. There are hundreds of Jewish writings and teachings about how to treat the body as a holy vessel that houses our soul and allows us to do good deeds and repair some aspect of the broken or unfinished world during our precious years on Earth.

So it naturally follows that when we prepare some food or we sit down to a meal or a snack, we aren't just hungry mammals who need instant gratification in a mindless way. It may look to an outsider like it's just you and the fork poking at the food. But from a Jewish perspective, the food is how we take good care of the holy vessel (the delicate body) that houses our soul and allows us to raise up our energy for taking care of our loved ones and having good energy for doing our part in the ongoing creation of the unfinished world.

From a Jewish perspective, we don't "own" our bodies and we don't have the right to mistreat or neglect our bodies. Rather, this holy vessel that houses your unique, individual, creative soul is on loan and needs to be cared for lovingly with excellent rest, activity, and nutrition because the Ever-flowing Source of Life is depending on you and me to be alert and healthy enough to act with patience and compassion in all sorts of challenging situations. Most importantly, the food is not just for us in isolation, but it's being given to us to keep our holy vessel in shape for doing some important acts of kindness, generosity, and creativity that might arise later this morning, this afternoon, and this evening.

There is a wonderful Kabbalah scholar, writer, and teacher who is alive in the 21st century named Rabbi Daniel Matt, who has described in profound ways how the act of eating a nutritious bite of food engages each of us as holy vessels for the daily process of raising up holy sparks of light and repairing the world one day at a time.

He writes, "You can mend the cosmos by anything you do—even eating. The purpose of eating is not just for mere pleasure or to fill the body. No, the purpose is about mending. When you eat or drink, and you focus your awareness on the love of God, then you elevate your physical desire to spiritual desire. Thereby you bring forth holy sparks from deep within the food, and you serve God."

In other words, the next time you sit down to a meal or a snack, consider for a moment whether you are eating only to fill your belly or whether you are also boosting your chances to do something patient, kind, creative or holy with this unique soul and this delicate body that you have responsibility to take care of during this lifetime.

As you look at the plate in front of you, are you willing to envision yourself as a loving, insightful, creative soul housed in a holy vessel that needs healthy nutritious fuel in order to do good deeds and be part of the ongoing healing and repair that is desperately needed? Are you willing to say a few words before eating so that you can remind your busy self of the possibilities for doing good that might emerge from this calming moment of re-fueling your holy vessel?

The Woman Who Thought She Was Too Busy to Have a Relaxed Meal

Here's a quick example of someone who made the shift from rushed, anxious eating and discovered the possibility of treating her body like a holy vessel that deserves loving care. Please see if Donna's brief story sounds like you or someone you know:

I met Donna several years ago at a seminar for parents of children with special needs. She and I have each been raising kids we love who are on the Autism Spectrum and we are always needing to learn more about how to help our kids do well in the world. In one of our conversations during a break between seminar sessions about the challenges of being a very-involved parent for a difficult-to-soothe child, Donna mentioned the fact that, "Before I was a mom, I used to kick back and enjoy a relaxing glass of wine and a delicious home-cooked meal. But lately I've cut out the wine because it makes me a little sleepy and I need to be at my best in order to deal with whatever my autistic son needs when he gets overwhelmed by things and I have to be fully present, calm and focused at those moments. I also haven't been cooking intricate meals or enjoying very many relaxed dinners or lunches lately because there just isn't time since I'm a single mom running a small business from home, plus taking care of a special needs son, and during any free moments I'm being an activist and advocate for my son and other special needs kids to make sure that the state, the voters, the teachers, and the school system do a better job of protecting the rights and accessibility for our kids."

Donna admitted, "I want to stay healthy and be there for my son, but I'm starting to feel worn down physically from rushing through meals, gobbling down a lot of unhealthy stuff because it's quick and available, and messing up my digestion from the way I've been eating lately."

For the next two years, I talked with Donna on the phone a few times about our kids navigating various school and social dilemmas and I also heard her expressing several times her concern that, "My life is so overloaded these days. I don't have the time or energy lately to focus on having a relaxed meal, yet I'm starting to feel lousy about my health and my looks from all the junk I've been eating."

I wasn't sure whether it was appropriate for me to offer any suggestions about food or digestion to Donna. She and I were primarily helping each other on issues that impacted our special needs kids, and she wasn't asking for my advice about other topics, especially something as private and personal as "What are your food habits lately."

But then something interesting happened. Donna told me in one of our phone calls that she was Jewish and mostly non-religious, and that a friend of hers who was both a licensed nutritionist and an adult education teacher at a nearby Jewish temple had invited her to one of her on-line Zoom classes on the topic of "Jewish Approaches to Self-Care and Healthy Eating."

In that eye-opening class, Donna's friend had taught her about the fascinating specifics of "treating your body as a holy vessel" and how to make sure that each day you give your body the self-care that will allow you to do more good deeds, for being energized and nourished enough to be fully present for your loved ones, and also to have the fuel you will need for repairing some aspect of the world that you know needs improvement.

As Donna explained, "I realized that the complicated and important things I do for my son and when I'm being an activist for the rights of other special needs kids—these are holy works and I need to start treating my body as a holy vessel to keep it healthy for doing good in the world, so that I don't burn out or become so run down that I can't keep doing this important work in a relaxed, compassionate way. Seeing from a Jewish spiritual perspective the way I would like to interact with food as being the fuel that allows me to do good deeds and make a difference for my son and other kids has changed the way I eat. I no longer grab the first easy junk food that tastes great but usually causes me to feel bloated or spacy. Lately I've been preparing quick but very nutritious meals for myself and my son. I began to realize I truly can do this in a healthy way, even though I'm still a very busy person. Plus, I've also begun to stop for a quiet minute before each meal or snack to check in with my body and relax the places that are feeling stressed or tight, and then I say a short prayer in my own words to ask for guidance and to offer thanks for this chance to regain my calmness and my strength for whatever is coming next that day."

If you (or someone you know) is like Donna and you have felt too overloaded to stop and give yourself a quiet moment before a healthy, nourishing meal, please ask yourself if you would be willing to experiment with one or two days of using a prayer before a meal or snack to unhook from the pressures for even just a few seconds. Your stomach and your intestines might thank you. The people in your life who need your calmness and your centered presence might thank you. In addition, you might feel a stronger connection to the flow of creation and repair that needs you to be part of the solutions to what is broken or unfinished in this world of ours. We need you to stay healthy because you are one of the forces for good. Please make sure you provide the self-care and the loving, gentle moments that your holy vessel needs in order to thrive.

Deepened Experience #3: Finding a Way to Share with Others the Delicious Sustenance That You Are Enjoying.

One final important aspect you might find interesting about food and Judaism is that we are taught to look beyond the food in front of us and consider for a moment the people nearby, as well as the people many miles away, who are having a much tougher time finding quality food to eat for themselves and their families. It's not about feeling guilty, but rather about asking in a Jewish way, "What can I do to be part of the solution?"

In Judaism, which cherishes life and being fully alive in so many ways, we are taught to enjoy and be grateful for each delicious bite of food that nourishes our soul and the soul of our loved ones. At the same time, we are taught to never forget that our ancestors were slaves, that many of our people in recent centuries have been hungry or struggling, and that we are capable of helping to relieve some of the suffering in the world today and assist in finding solutions to the economic injustices and environmental destructiveness that we see all around us. In Judaism it's about balance and keeping your heart open—that no matter whether we are rich, middle-income, or barely scraping by, we can raise up our energy as often as possible by giving a little something to heal the planet and make life better for someone else as well.

Every year at Passover gatherings in Jewish homes and congregations, there is a prayer before the meal that says, "Let all who are hungry come and eat." But in order to live up to that prayer, we each might need to increase our knowledge of exactly how many people are hungry and what we can do to make sure they get good, nutritious food to eat and clean water to drink. So for a moment, let's look at the facts together:

I didn't fully realize it until I looked it up recently, but according to several major surveys and extensive research in the past few years, it is now estimated that over forty-five million individuals in the United States are in households that are "food insecure." Either because of unemployment, or low-wage employment, or lack of access to quality foods (which can be life-or-death for someone with diabetes or other food-related challenges), these forty-five million Americans wake up each day feeling unsure of whether they will have enough to eat or a decent amount of nutrition for themselves or their children.

Forty-five million might sound like just a number. But what if we tried to imagine for a moment how many individual human beings that would be. On the one hand, it would be enough people to fill up 450 enormous 100,000 seating-capacity football stadiums side by side. Or the number "forty-five million people who are unsure about being able to afford nutritious food" could also be understood as "more people than the number of individuals who live in New York State, or in Florida, or in Texas."

Now let's get personal for a moment so that this startling fact begins to feel more motivating than just a random number. Have you in your own most difficult moments ever been "food insecure" and unable to count on a decent, nutritious meal? Or have your parents, grandparents, or great grandparents ever had to "make do" on less than what they needed to be decently fed? I think of my own paternal grandparents when they were in Auschwitz hoping to stay alive with just a portion of a potato or a sip of tasteless soup. Or my maternal grandparents when they lived in a small town in Eastern Europe during an especially difficult economic downturn.

What about your family? Are there stories and memories of being hungry or being very anxious about how to put food on the table for their kids and their elders?

One Fascinating Verse That Can Inspire Your Efforts

In Judaism, we are encouraged to "pray with your feet," which means to choose and follow through on some action that can begin to make a difference in something that is painfully wrong or unfair. When you think about Judaism, food, and living a compassionate life, there is a particular teaching that I have found to be one of my favorite paragraphs from the Torah about taking action to help those who are hungry or going through a tough time in their lives. It's an intriguing suggestion in Leviticus chapter 19, verse 9 where it says, "When you gather the harvest of your land, you shall not gather all the way to the edges of your field, or gather the gleanings of your harvest, or pick your vineyard bare, or gather the fallen fruit of your vineyard. You shall leave them for the poor and the stranger…"

Now if you read that paragraph once or twice carefully, what does it stir up in you? Especially if you are not a farmer with a vineyard, what does the suggestion to "leave the gleanings of the field and the fallen fruit for the poor and the stranger" mean to you personally?

Here are several possible ways that Jewish scholars and everyday folks have interpreted this crucial suggestion for "praying with your feet" and doing something big or small about hunger and suffering:

- Some say this paragraph about "leaving the edges of your field for the poor and the stranger" means essentially that you should always make sure to donate a portion of what you harvest, or a portion of what you earn, or a portion of what you are given as a gift, or a portion of what you do in your creative work life, to share with people who are struggling or insecure about food or shelter or opportunities to stay afloat. Maybe that means giving around 10% of your earnings to charities that help people. Maybe it means doing pro bono (for the good of others) free or low-fee services where you make sure each year you give 10% of your time for sharing your gifts and talents with low-income clients or colleagues who aren't asked to pay what others can afford to pay. Maybe that means donating your unused food (from your large refrigerator or pantry, or from a party or celebration you host) to a place that feeds the hungry or the homeless.

- Some say the important essence of the line "leave the edges of your field for the poor and the stranger" is that we need to think creatively and find a do-able method to leave the extra food and other donations in a less-shaming way so that some individual or family with economic insecurity can pick up the fallen fruit or reach for the unpicked good stuff (for which we have an excess amount) and they won't feel ashamed or exposed, but rather they can pick some delicious items or benefit from the donations in a respectful, confidential way. If the extra food or fruit is left along the adjacent trail "at the edge of your field" or at a convenient site where no one has to trespass onto private property to be able to feed their loved ones, then no one has to feel "watched" or "found out." What a beautiful, compassionate teaching—that the Torah and Jewish tradition are encouraging us, "Be creative, do well in your heartfelt projects and work life, and somehow find a way to let others have a portion of your abundance, your gifts, and your food—and do it in a way where they don't get exposed, embarrassed, or diminished as a respected human being."

- Some say the words "leave the edges of your field for the poor and the stranger" actually means don't close off your own heart and be locking away or making inaccessible all the food you are able to afford, or anxiously hoarding all the abundance that you have achieved, but rather to be a little less anxious and a little more generous as a result of being aware that giving away 10% of what you have still allows you to provide for yourself and your family with 90%.

- Some say the words "leave the edges of your field for the poor and the stranger" is a reminder that we don't own the Earth and all of its abundance, but rather that the nutritious elements of the Earth are loaned to us so that we can feed our loved ones and others, but to do it in a way that gets replenished and renewed for future generations. From a Jewish perspective, we are stewards or guardians who have a chance to enjoy the fruits of creation but also to restore and rebuild so that others can enjoy it as well.

All of these mindful, caring, and extremely-practical teachings come from that one intriguing phrase, "Leave the edges of your field for the poor and the stranger." As many have said about the Torah, "turn it over and turn it over because everything is contained in it."

As you think about your own life, do you sometimes feel power-less and guilty about the amount of hunger, homelessness, polluted water resources, famines, droughts, floods, and suffering that you see on the news or on your travels to and from your home? Do you sometimes feel as if, "There's not much that one person can do to make a dent?"

If your heart feels stirred up when you see so much suffering in the world, then your prayer of thanks "for the food that comes from the Earth" can be a wake-up call that you are ready to do at least one small action that is constructive and useful for reducing the amount of suffering for families and children near and far. Here are just a few small and realistic steps that you (or a loved one) can do to be part of the solutions instead of just being overwhelmed by the problems. See which of the following you want to explore immediately, or in the next few weeks, or in the next year, either on your own or with your congregation or group of friends:

- After saying a prayer and enjoying a good meal, ask yourself, "Is there a Jewish charity I can contribute to once a week, or once a month, or once a year that is helping to reduce the amount of food insecurity, hunger, and homelessness in my city, in my country, or in the world at large?" Or ask yourself, "Am I ready to be part of a group that shows up for some vol-unteer time slots for helping people who are struggling with food insecurity and financial setbacks?" Be sure to explore, "What is a reasonable amount of money donation or volunteer hours that won't jeopardize your own personal financial stability or cause you to lose sight of your other important priorities? What is the healthy and balanced amount for you personally between 'I've been doing or giving a little too much' and 'I'm probably doing or giving less than I could be doing or giving?'" Sometimes it takes a few attempts before we find that balanced amount of how much donated time or money allows us to not become burned out and yet we are able to give our fair share.

- If you have felt sad or concerned when you've seen reports on the news about hunger and food shortages locally or globally, there is another do-able option that you might want to consider. Either today or sometime this week, or this month, when you take a moment after saying a prayer and enjoying a good meal, you can ask yourself, "Am I part of the problem or part of the solution as to some of the underlying causes of what is triggering rising temperatures that destroy crops, or that cause pollution of essential rivers, lakes, and oceans, or that result in other environmental problems that increase the extent of hunger locally or globally?"

In many Jewish communities for the past few decades, there is an uplifting speaker and writer named Rabbi Ellen Bernstein and an organization called "Shomrei Adamah, Keepers of the Earth," that help individuals, families and congregations to learn about the Jewish spiritual teachings and the specific actions that we can start doing right away to begin to repair the planet, reduce the chances of famines, floods, pollution, and food shortages, so that we can find realistic ways to reduce the human suffering and hunger that comes as a result of our misguided environmental practices. In her books "Ecology and the Jewish Spirit: Where Nature and the Sacred Meet," "The Promise of the Land: A Passover Haggadah," and "Let the Earth Teach You Torah," she spells out what each of us can do to increase our awareness and find realistic steps for being better caretakers of the Earth and the human impact that results from how we mistreat the Earth.

One of the things I appreciate about Rabbi Ellen Bernstein is that she builds bridges of understanding and teamwork between the many secular environmentalists who are uncomfortable with some of the spiritual terminologies, as well as the many spiritual/religious environmentalists who are uncomfortable with some of the secular viewpoints. Instead of being at odds with one another, she helps them work together toward healing the planet and improving the chances for making sure everyone will have sufficient nutritious food, breathable air, and drinkable water now and in the future.

- As one additional option for addressing your heartfelt concerns about hunger and food insecurity locally or globally, you might consider after saying a prayer and enjoying a good meal that you can ask yourself, "Is there some organization that I want to support by doing something real and practical (with my family, or my group of friends, or my congregation) to help reduce the violence and social disruptions that worsen the level of food insecurity for millions of people near or far?"

You might be surprised at how many Jews and others are involved in coming up with innovative ways to help people who are food insecure as a result of the violence and political instability they are living with daily. You and I don't have to come up with the innovative solutions, but we can help those who are making a crucial difference.

For example, I remember a few years ago, my daughter was in a class at a congregation where they worked with the remarkable organization Jewish World Watch (that is devoted to preventing genocides and cruelty around the world) to put together colorful, sturdy backpacks of easy-to-utilize, portable, solar-powered cooking stoves and supplies for over 10,000 women in two war-torn countries in Africa where many women had been raped, robbed, or beaten up when they traveled to cities to buy food for their families. But now with these 10,000 donated, hand-painted backpacks with solar-powered cooking devices (created and sent from thousands of Jewish kids working as occasional volunteers for Jewish World Watch), these at-risk women could transport and cook foods much closer to home, have more time to start their own local businesses, and stay safe while taking better care of themselves and their families.

In addition, there are many Jewish organizations that are committed to peace and resolving the tensions between clashing groups (that often cause economic upheavals and increasing levels of hunger) in various parts of the world. Many of these Jewish organizations help to get food and essential resources to families and children who have become refugees because of violence and disruptions in their home countries. My dad (and several other relatives and counseling clients of mine) were helped enormously by Jewish organizations including the American Joint Distribution Committee, the Hebrew Immigrant Aid Society, and the American Jewish World Service. Each of these non-profits not only help Jews in distress, but also people of all races, religions, and ethnicities.

By giving money or a little bit of volunteer time to these groups, you not only save lives and feed families during a crisis, but you also raise up your own sense of being a light unto the nations and repairing the world one small act of kindness at a time. Every year at Passover, we tell the story of Shifra and Puah, the two Egyptian women who risked their lives to save Jewish children who were about to be killed. Every year in our own lives, we have the chance to help others that we might never meet in person and yet their hunger and their lives can be transformed somewhat by the actions we take during a moment of saying, "Thank you Eternal Source for the food that comes from the Earth." I am anticipating that each year, we can continue to connect with these and other Jewish organizations that are coming up with innovative ways to be part of the creative solutions to hunger and homelessness, and not just be overwhelmed by the size of the problems.

Sharing What You Have Been Learning

I hope this chapter and this book have given you and your loved ones a glimpse into how to connect your daily life with the inspiring words of prayer, meditation, and moment-by-moment centering and mindfulness that can be found in key Jewish phrases that have profound implications. My hope is that at least one of these eight chapters will assist you and strengthen you whenever you need a boost to raise up your energy and express your creative, compassionate self. I also hope you will share some of these uplifting words and their deeper meanings with the people in your life who have felt estranged from Jewish spirituality or unsure of what the Hebrew words mean.

But please be respectful of whatever hesitations or concerns your friends or loved ones have (and don't try to force anything on anyone). These profound and holy words are intended for doing good in the world and lifting us up during moments when we are feeling overloaded, fragmented, or pulled in several directions at once. I hope they will help you and many of your loved ones this year and during the upcoming years. Thank you for all that you do to support and inspire so many people in your corner of the world. I pray that you and your loved ones will continue to be a force for good for many, many years to come.

Discussion Questions

Have you ever had a wonderful conversation about what really matters in the big picture, or about the things that are most challenging in your life right now, and you came away from that particular discussion saying, "Wow, that was time well spent!"

Each of the chapters of this book "How These Words Can Raise Up Your Energy" are intended to open up meaningful conversations about important Jewish topics that have real-life implications. If possible within your busy schedule, please find a way to connect more personally with each of these very helpful Jewish prayers and centering methods by using specific portions of this book as the spark for some profound and honest conversations.

Whether you pair up with one engaging discussion partner for some deep talks, or if you participate in an inspiring class or book group at a congregation you like (either in person or on your computer screen), here are some open-ended questions you can choose from:

Chapter 1: What Does It Mean to Listen Deeply?

- Describe a moment you remember from recently or long ago when you got very quiet, listened carefully, and possibly felt a sense of connection or "oneness" in nature, or in a prayer service, or in a soul-to-soul conversation with another human being. What does "oneness" or "deep connection" feel like to you when it happens?

- What is your preferred way of translating and interpreting the Sh'ma? From the several possible versions described by the author in Chapter One, which version appeals to you personally and what did you experience when you utilized that particular interpretation?

- Describe a moment when you were anxious (or feeling alienated or separate) during the daytime or late at night, and then you said the Sh'ma and it re-opened a flow of energy, support, or insight that shifted your mood noticeably.

- Describe a moment when you truly listened deeply (sh'ma) to someone who was upset or curious…and this willingness to listen with an open heart was healing or helpful for one or both of you.

Chapter 2: How Do You Get from Tiredness to Gratitude?

- Even if you are having a stressful day or a tough week, what is something large or small for which you feel thankful or grateful right at this moment?

- Have you ever said first thing in the morning that you are appreciative for your soul being renewed for a new day and that you are open to doing something meaningful or helpful that day? How did this prayerful moment affect your decisions and your actions later that day (and how long did the good energy and forward momentum last before you needed a booster dose from an additional prayer or meditation phrase)?

- What is your personal way of helping your body to stay healthy and unblocked on a stressful day so that you can say a prayer of gratitude a little while later on to feel thankfulness for how well your complicated body is working right now (despite everything)?

- In this chapter the author describes several different versions of the prayer phrase, "Thank you for making firm my steps." What are the specific steps or journeys in your life (now or in the past) for which you sometimes need careful awareness, guidance, or support so that your steps are firm?

Chapter 3: Would You Like to Experience "a Great Love" More Often?

- In what ways do you feel nourished or "loved" by what you have received from a mysterious Source of Life or the hard-to-describe universal flow?

- Describe a moment when you felt disconnected or "falling out of love" with God or the Infinite Source (and what steps have you taken thus far to find a way to reconnect).

- If you were going to write a thank you note, or a poem, or a personal journal entry, or a loving lyric to the One who breathed life into you and who is continually flowing in your direction, what would you say?

- Is there someone you care about who has felt estranged or somewhat divorced from God or Judaism? What have you discovered is the reason why some people drift away from the search for a Divine Presence and what tends to open up some people to renew their search?

Chapter 4: Starting a Conversation About Important Topics

- If you were going to have an honest and genuine one-on-One conversation with the Creative Source of All That Exists, what would you like to say and hear?

- What does it feel like for you when you go up on your tiptoes to say "Kadosh, Kadosh, Kadosh, Holy, Holy, Holy," and what might be some of the ways in your daily life that you are attempting to be one of the angels, or agents, or messengers, for the Creative Source?

- The beginning of the Standing Prayer talks about the blessings that come from our ancestors. Who in your family tree (either in the past 100 years or going as far back as Abraham and Sarah) inspired you and what did this person teach you or give you?

- The middle of the Standing Prayer has a suggestion that we will share our Judaism and our most cherished values "L'dor va-dor, from generation to generation." As you think about a younger friend or sibling of yours, or if you someday will have (or already have) kids or grandchildren, nieces or nephews, how do you want to share your Judaism and what things would you do differently from how it was shared with you?

Chapter 5: What Happens When You Pray for Healing?

- What was it like for you when you sincerely prayed for healing for yourself or a loved one?

- In Chapter Five, the author discusses the difference between two translations—refu'ah sh'layma as "complete healing" or refu'ah sh'layma as "a renewal of wholeness." When have you experienced a "renewal of wholeness" even when there were still some symptoms or challenges still ahead for you or the person you were praying for?

- What is a charity or an organization you recommend as a way to bring healing to a situation that you or a loved one have faced?

- If you were to pray for healing and say the phrase "I am in your hands," would you tend to think of human hands who are agents of healing, or do you think of natural elements that are created for healing, or do you envision God intervening directly, or do you seek a combination of each?

Chapter 6: How the Kaddish Works on Many Levels

- When have you felt comforted by the Kaddish and when have you felt confused about the Kaddish?

- What is your personal belief about the journey of the soul after a person has died?

- Have you ever felt extremely sad or distant from the world, or from the flow of life, after the death of someone you loved (and how long did it take before you began to notice again some of the beauty and goodness in the world)?

- What are the words or actions you wanted from people when you were in grief, and what are the words or actions that were not helpful or comfortable for you?

Chapter 7: How to Increase the Inner and the Outer Lights

- Describe a moment from recent weeks or long ago when you were fascinated by watching the candle flames dancing and moving.

- What is your most favorite part of Shabbat and what is your least favorite part of Shabbat?
- What is your particular way of making the Sabbath meal, the Shabbat candle lighting, or the Shabbat day, special and unlike the other days of the week?
- If you could imagine a time when the world is healed and everyone has enough food, justice, love, and joy, what would that be like? What is one thing you are doing (or would like to do) to make this healed world a reality?

Chapter 8: What Makes Each Meal More Meaningful?

- Describe a time when you said a prayer before a meal and it helped your body relax or it improved the taste of what you were eating?
- What are the foods and beverages that bring out the best in you, and what are the foods and beverages that cause problems for you?
- What is your personal way of making sure that others who are "food insecure" or under-nourished can have sufficient food and nutrients?
- When have you thought of your body as a "holy vessel" and what is your particular way of taking good care of that holy vessel?

Notes and Source

Chapter One: What Does It Mean to Listen Deeply?
"The brief Sh'ma phrase..."

It can be found originally in the Book of Deuteronomy, chapter 6, verse 4, and in nearly every Jewish prayer book for weekdays, Shabbats, and holidays.

"The shhhhh sound of the first word of the Sh'ma..."

I didn't invent the idea of meditating gently on the soft shhhh sound of Sh'ma. I've seen several rabbis and cantors suggest this meditation method and I first heard it from Rabbi David Cooper in 1991 at a Shabbat service he was leading at Makom Ohr Shalom in Los Angeles.

"The Shekhinah or In-Dwelling Presence..."

For more on the Jewish concept of an Indwelling Presence that is either feminine or non-gendered, please see "Shekhinah: The Divine Feminine" at www.myjewishlearning.com or "Shekhinah The Dwelling," at www.jewishencyclopedia.com, or "The Shekhinah: Two Faces: "Aspects of the Divine," by Rabbi Jill Hammer, at www. telshemesh.org

"Wrestling with God..."

For more on the Jewish concept of wrestling or striving with the Divine Presence, please see

"Israel Means to Struggle with God," by Fred Claar, at www.my-jewishlearning.com or "Wrestling with God," by Rabbi Elliot Dorff, at www.aju.edu

"An intimate conversation between two study partners or two sweet souls…"

For more on the Jewish concept of "Hevruta," study partners who are friends and who challenge one another, please see "Havruta: Learning in Pairs," by Rachael Gelfman Schultz, at www.myjewish-learning.com

"It actually says, 'Yud Hei Vov Hei…"

For more on the Jewish concept of the Divine as "Yud Hei Vov Hei, what is, what was, and what will be," please see "What is the Tetragrammaton," (adapted from The Jewish Encyclopedia) at www.myjewishlearning.com or "Yud Hei Vov Hei: God's Name is a Four Letter Word" by Rabbi Paul Kipnes, at www.reformjudaism.org

"When Moses says to the Divine Source, 'What should I call You' and the Infinite Voice says 'Ehi-yeh Ah-sheir Ehi-yeh, I am becoming what I am becoming…"

This conversation can be found originally in The Book of Exodus, chapter 3, verses 13-15. For more on the Jewish concept of God as an ever-flowing, continually evolving Source, please see "Who is this God Ehyeh-Asher-Ehyeh" by Rabbi Peter Knobel, at www.reform-judaism.org or "A Guide to Understanding God as Process," compiled by Susan Berrin, Sh'ma Now: A Journal of Jewish Sensibilities, May 31, 2019, quoted in The Forward at www.forward.com

or in the book "Ehyeh Asher Ehyeh: The Name of God," by David Birnbaum and Martin S. Cohen, New York: Mesorah Matrix Books, 2019.

"The opening paragraph of the Great Prayer has a repetition of 'God of this person' and 'God of that person'..."

For more on the Jewish concept that each person has a different experience and clue about the Divine Source, please see "The Weekly Siddur" by B.S. Jacobson, Tel Aviv: Sinai Press, 1978, p. 215, or "My People's Prayer Book: The Amidah," by Rabbi Lawrence Hoffman, Nashville, TN: Jewish Lights, 2014, p. 70, or "What's in a Name?" by Lauren Eichler Berkun, January 4, 2003 at Jewish Theological Seminary, www.jts.edu

"Marie Kondo..."

Also known as Konmari, she is the author of four books on tidiness, organizing, and reducing clutter.

"Dr. Marcia Falk..."

For more on her writings about prayer and Jewish spirituality, please see "The Book of Blessings," San Francisco: Harper, 1996, and "The Days Between," Waltham, MA: Brandeis University Press, 2014.

"Rabbi David Cooper..."

The two books written by Rabbi David Cooper that are referred to in this chapter are "The Heart of Stillness," New York: Bell Tower, 1992, and "God is a Verb," New York: Riverhead, 1997.

"A coming together of Judaism and scientific research..."

For more about the respect for science in Judaism, please see "Why Judaism Embraces Science," by Rabbi Geoffrey Mitelman, July 21, 2012 at www.sciencereligiondialogue.org, or "Integrating Science and Religion: A Jewish Perspective," by Norbert Samuelson, at www.bu.edu, or "Science and Religion in Modern Jewish Thought," by Shalom Rosenberg, 2015, Bloomington: Indiana University Press, at www.jstor.org, or "Judaism and Science in History" at www.myjewishlearning.com, or "How Has Jewish Thought Influenced Science?" January-February 2014, at www.momentmag.com

"Rabbi Isaac Luria and the Big Bang Theory..."

For more on the similarities between what was said in Tzefat 500 years ago and what was said in science in the past 80 years, please see "Kabbalah, Science and the Creation of the Universe," by Nathan Aviezer, Fall 2004, at www.jewishaction.com or "First Constriction: Introduction to the Ari's Concept of 'Tzimtzum' by Moshe Miller, at www.chabad.org

"The Jew in the Lotus"

For more on the dialogues in India between Jewish rabbis who teach meditation and the Dalai Lama from Tibet who wanted to learn about keeping a spiritual people alive while in exile, please see "The Jew in the Lotus: A Poet's Rediscovery of Jewish Identity in Buddhist India," by Rodger Kamenetz, New York: Harper Collins, 1994.

Chapter Two: How Do You Get from Tiredness to Gratitude?

"Scientific proof that the human brain is hard-wired to look for problems, incompletions..."

This research is described in "On Finished and Unfinished Tasks," by Bluma Zeigarnik, in the book "A Source Book of Gestalt Psychology," 1938, pages 300-314, and in "Unfinished Tasks Foster Rumination and Impair Sleeping," by CJ Syrek, Journal of Occupational Health, 2014, volume 19, issue 4, pages 490-499, and in The International Encyclopedia of the Social Sciences, volume 5, p. 407.

"The Path of Blessing..."

This approach to spiritual practice is described in the book "The Path of Blessing" by Rabbi Marcia Prager, Woodstock, Vermont: Jewish Lights, 2003, and in the book "Stalking Elijah," by Rodger Kamenetz, New York: Harper, 1997, and in the book review "The Path of Blessing" by Rabbi Rachel Barenblat, December 27, 2004, found at www.velveteenrabbi.blogs.com

"Modah/Modeh/Modet Ahnee…"

This morning prayer can be found in the Talmud, Berachot 60b and its history is described in "The Encyclopedia of Jewish Prayer," by Macy Nulman, Northvale, New Jersey: Jason Aronson Books, 1996, p. 251.

"Modet and non-gendered pronouns…"

The gender non-binary version of Modet Ahnee is described in "Modeh Ani" by Rabbi Vivie Mayer, at www.ritualwell.org, and in "Gender Neutral Hebrew," by Hannah Steinkopf-Frank, at www. them.us and at www.nonbinaryhebrew.com

"I have found that diverse people from many religions appreciate this early-morning prayer…"

Since 2001 when I wrote about this focusing prayer of gratitude in "Seven Prayers That Can Change Your Life" I have received numerous phone calls, emails, and letters from individuals from many spiritual and religious traditions saying that they are using this Jewish prayer and that it helps them significantly.

"The Birkhat Ahsheir Yatzar, the blessing for how the body works as well as it does…"

Originally found in the Talmud, Berachot 60b, the history of this prayer is described in "The Encyclopedia of Jewish Prayer," by Macy Nulman, Northvale, New Jersey: Jason Aronson Books, 1996, page 42, and in "Finding God Through the Body" by Rabbi Myriam Klotz, at www.myjewishlearning.com

"Rabbi Abaye…"

His story and the origins of his prayer for the body can be found in the Talmud, Berachot 60b page 120, and in "Abaye," www.ou.org/leaders-in-the-talmudic-period and at "Abbaye," by Nissan Mendel, at www.chabad.org

"The Birkhat Ha-Shakhar morning blessings…"

Their history and intricacies are described in "The Encyclopedia of Jewish Prayer," by Macy Nulman, Northvale, New Jersey: Jason Aronson Books, 1996, pages 115-117.

"Rabbi Marcia Prager…"

Her writings and teachings are described at www.marciaprager.com and at www.pnaior-phila.org in the section "our rabbi-chaver."

"July 2011 Jewish spiritual conference in Redlands, California…"

This was a week-long summer retreat or "Kallah" sponsored by Aleph, the Alliance for Jewish Renewal, and open to all branches of Judaism.

"Watch the rabbi tie the shoes…"

There is a story in the Talmud (Berachot 62a) about a student who desperately wanted to learn how the rabbi acts in everyday life, down to the details of how the rabbi tied shoes, and so the student hid under the rabbi's bed.

"Gilda Radner's funny character would likely say…"

On "Saturday Night Live" from 1975 to 1977, Gilda Radner (from my hometown of Detroit) had a recurring character named Emily Litella who would get very upset and rant at something in the news she mis-heard (such as "What's All the Fuss About Saving Soviet Jewelry") and then when it was explained to her she would calm down and reply, "Never mind."

"One of the rabbinic interpretations of 'clothe the naked' as generosity and dignity…"

For more on the Jewish teachings about making sure people have dignity from wearing donated quality clothing, please see "A Close Look at Birkot Hashachar," by Rabbi Ed Gelb, July 1, 2016, at www.campramah.org or "Clean Clothes and Our Souls," by Jackie Headapohl and Rabbi Dan Horwitz, February 1, 2018, in The Detroit Jewish News at www.thejewishnews.com or "The Naked and the Nude" by Rabbi Bradley Shavit Artson, at www.aju.edu or "The Orthodox Jewish Woman Who Started an Organization to Clothe People with Dignity," by Eric Goldstein at www.jewinthecity.com

"The National Council of Jewish Women…"

For more about their programs and how to donate clothes at their thrift stores, please see www.ncjw.org

"Another way of interpreting 'clothing the naked' is the teachings that keep us from being unprotected or susceptible…"

For more on the spiritual interpretations of "clothing the naked," please see "Putting on Soul Garments" by Shaul Yosef Leiter at www.chabad.org

"The quote from Michelle Obama…"

For more on her 2016 speech and what it means in practical terms, please see "Transcript: Read Michelle Obama's Full Speech," July 26, 2016, at www.washingtonpost.com or "Opinion: Michelle Obama Still 'Going High' When They Go Low," August 17, 2020 at www.LATimes.com or "Michelle Obama on What 'Going High' Means Today," August 18, 2020 at www.cnbc.com

"One hundred blessings…"

The origin of this practice might be that we needed 100 silver beams to construct the foundation bases of the tabernacle in Exodus chapter 39, verse 27 and so we need 100 blessings to construct a strong foundation each day as described in the Talmud, Menachot 43b and in Tur Orach Chaim #46. Or it might be that when 100 people died per day during a plague at the time of King David, it was suggested as a remedy that we say 100 blessings or thank you's each day to be strengthened against illness or plagues, according to the Midrash Bamidbar Rabba, Parshas Korach 12 and 18. Or it might be a modern way of staying appreciative even on tough days, as described in "One Hundred Blessings: An Attitude of Gratitude," by Dr. Alissa Zuchman, Bureau of Jewish Education, Chicago, at www.jteach.org

"Rabbi Miriam Hamrell's Mussar study group..."

For 18 years I've been a participant each Saturday morning at 9 a.m. at a Mussar (ethics or character growth) discussion group where we look at Jewish teachings on how to stay centered, balanced, and compassionate in all sorts of daily real-life challenges. For more information about Mussar classes, see www.ahavattorahla.org or www.mussarinstitute.org or "What Is Mussar?" by Greg Marcus, at www.myjewishlearning.com

Chapter Three: Would You Like to Experience 'the Great Love' More Often?

"Love songs that sound like 'I hope you don't mind that I put down in words...'"

This is the well-known lyric from "Your Song" by Elton John and Bernie Taupin, 1970, produced by Gus Dudgeon, Uni DJM Records.

"Rabbi Debra Orenstein..."

She is a rabbi at Congregation B'nai Israel in Emerson, New Jersey and formerly was the rabbi at Makom Ohr Shalom in Los Angeles and an instructor at American Jewish University. Her books include "Lifecycles 1: Jewish Women on Life Passages and Personal Milestones." For more information, see www.rabbidebra.com

"Ahavah Rabbah (the Great Love)..."

This prayer can be found in most Ashkenazic morning prayers books for weekdays, holidays and Sabbaths (and in both the morning and evening Sephardic prayer books). It is described in historical and procedural ways in "The Encyclopedia of Jewish Prayer," by Macy Nulman, Northvale, New Jersey: Jason Aronson Books, 1993, pages 11-12.

"Indication #2: That the 'Great Love' is the Instruction Guidance from a higher source..."

In the Talmud (Berachot 11b and 12a) and in the Mishnah (Tamid 5:1), it says God's love and kindness are evident in giving us the Torah and guidance on how to live a meaningful life. In the Kol Bo, chapter 8 (a collection of Jewish ritual laws), it describes God's love as being expressed through the written and oral Torah teachings.

"A very patient and wise rabbi in my hometown of Detroit..."

I grew up at Temple Israel in Detroit where I had numerous one-on-one conversations with Rabbi M. Robert Syme, of blessed memory.

"Ahavat Olam (the everlasting love)..."

This prayer can be found in most evening prayer books for weekdays, holidays, and Sabbaths. It is described in historical and procedural ways in "The Encyclopedia of Jewish Prayer," by Macy Nulman, Northvale, New Jersey: Jason Aronson Books, 1993, page 12.

"Rabbi Anson Laytner..."

From Seattle, Washington, he has spent many years as a hospice chaplain and is the author of several books on Jewish-Chinese relations, along with the book "Arguing with God," Northvale, New Jersey: Jason Aronson Books, 1998.

"Rabbi Harold Schulweis…"

He was the rabbi for many years at Valley Beth Shalom in Encino, California and was the co-founder of the Jewish Foundation for the Righteous (to support non-Jews who saved Jews during the Holocaust) and Jewish World Watch (to support human rights and prevent genocides around the world). His books include "For Those Who Can't Believe: Overcoming the Obstacles to Faith," New York: Harper Collins, 1994.

"Touring red states and blue states for The Ten Challenges…"

This book, which explored the psychological aspects and the practical steps of understanding and utilizing the Ten Utterances or the Ten Commandments, was published in 1997 by Crown/Harmony in New York and re-issued in 2004 by Sheffield Publishing in Salem, Wisconsin.

"Tevye in Fiddler on the Roof…"

The character Tevye the Dairyman was created by Sholem Aleichem (Solomon Naumovich Rabinovich) in a series of short stories and adapted in the 1964 musical "Fiddler on the Roof," written by Jerry Bock, Sheldon Harnick, and Joseph Stein.

"Hear from Elie Wiesel…"

His essay "A Prayer for the Days of Awe" was printed in the Opinion section of The New York Times on October 2, 1997 and reprinted in Jewish newspapers around the world in 1998 and 1999.

"Numerous Jewish writers and scholars have suggested that the Creator intentionally made room for human free will, randomness, and some imperfections…"

For more on Jewish rabbis and writers who describe the world as having some randomness and unpredictability, please see "Jewish Theology and Process Thought," by Sandra Lubarsky and David Ray Griffin, Stony Brook, New York: SUNY Press, 1996, or "God of Becoming and Relatedness," by Rabbi Bradley Shavit Artson, Woodstock, Vermont: Jewish Lights, 2016, or "Was God in the Earthquake?" by Rabbi Harold Schulweis, January 28, 1994 in the Jewish Journal of Los Angeles, also found at www.vbs.org

"Unhelpful folks in the U.S. State Department..."

For more on this painful episode, please see "State Department Obstruction Exposed," from the US Holocaust Memorial Museum at www.exhibitions.UShmm.org or "America and the Holocaust" at www.facinghistory.org or "American Political Leaders and Their Reponses to the Holocaust," from the Museum of Jewish Heritage, at www.mjhnyc.org

"Unhelpful folks in the British government..."

For more about this painful episode, please see "Immigration to Israel: British Restrictions on Jewish Immigration to Palestine," at www.jewishvirtuallibrary.org or "Uncovered, Polish Jews Pre-Holocaust Plea to Chamberlain: Let Us Into Palestine," by Steven Zipperstein, at www.timesofisrael.com

"Maybe I'm Amazed..."

This song was written by Paul McCartney, Sony/ATV Music Publishing, 1970.

"Taylor Swift, Del-i-cate..."

This song was written by Taylor Swift, Big Machine Records, 2018.

"Kol ha-neshahmah t'hah-leil Yah..."

This final line of Psalm 150 is described in "The Encyclopedia of Jewish Prayer," by Macy Nulman, Northvale, New Jersey: Jason Aronson Books, 1993, pages 150-151, and in the book "More Fully Alive" by Leonard Felder, Los Angeles: JFuture Books, 2016, pages 1-20.

Chapter Four: Starting a Conversation About Important Topics

"The Amidah (the Standing Prayer)…"

This prayer is described in depth in the book "My People's Prayer Book, Volume 2: The Amidah" by Rabbi Lawrence Hoffman, Woodstock, Vermont: Jewish Lights, 1998.

"On the Chabad site it says 'the Amidah is the centerpiece'…"

This can be found at "What is the Amidah?" and "The Weekly Amidah—Standing Before God" at www.chabad.org

"Many Conservative rabbis describe the Amidah as…"

This can be found in the Siddur prayer book "Sim Shalom," edited by Rabbi Jules Harlow, 1985, or in "The Imahot (Matriarchs) in the Amidah," by Rabbi Steve Wernick, at www.beth-tzedec.org

"Many Reform and Reconstructionist Jewish rabbis describe the Amidah as…"

This can be found at "Amidah," www.reformjudaism.org, or in "A Contemporary Amidah," by Rabbi Sheila Pelz Weinberg, at www.evolve.reconstructingjudaism.org

"Just like Hannah…"

Her intense prayer is described in 1st Samuel, chapter 1, verse 13, and in "Hannah as a Precedent-Setter," by Leora Jackson, Jewish Women's Archive, at www.jwa.org, or in "A Woman's Silent Prayer," by Rachel Kravetz, at www.jewishweek.timesofisrael.com, or in "Hannah's Prayer and Ours" by Rabbi Jeff Goldwasser, at www.rebjeff.com

"Rabbi Simcha Bunim Bonhardt…"

For more on the saying "Every person should have two pockets…," please see "Anavah, Humility Texts," at www.jewishcamp.org, or "Hands in Both Pockets," by Joe Laur, at www.todaysrabbi.com

"Kadosh, kadosh, kadosh comes from a vision by the prophet Isaiah..."

This was originally written in the Book of Isaiah, chapter 6, verse 3. Some interpretations can be found in "Kadosh, Kadosh, Kadosh" by Shir Yaakov, www.kolhai.org or in "Kedushah," by Rabbi Shefa Gold, at www.rabbishefagold.com

"Angels in Judaism..."

The concept of "angels" or "messengers" are explored in "Jewish Concepts: Angels and Angelology," at www.jewishvirtuallibrary.org, and in "The Power and Protection of Angels," by Ellen Umansky, at www.reformjudaism.org or in "Do Jews Believe in Angels" by Rabbi Amy Perlin, February 17, 2012 Sermon at Temple B'nai Shalom, Fairfax Station, Virginia, at www.tbs-online.org

"In the Talmud it says in the Standing Prayer there must be at least one personal prayer..."

This is described in Shulchan Aruch 119:1 and Mishna Berurah 119:1 and in "Adding Personal Requests to Daily Prayers," by Rabbi Dovid Rosenfeld, at www.aish.com and in "How to Talk to God," by Rabbi David Jaffe at www.myjewishlearning.com and in "Amidah Tensions" by Rabbi Rachel Barenblat, at www.velveteenrabbi.blogs.com

"Rabbi David Ellenson quoted in Rabbi Lawrence Hoffman's book..."

This can be found on page 128 of "My People's Prayer Book Volume 2: The Amidah" by Rabbi Lawrence Hoffman, Nashville, Tennessee: Jewish Lights, 1998.

"In the 1975, 1995 and 2007 revised prayer books..."

This refers to the Reform prayers books "Gates of Prayer" (1975), edited by Rabbi Chaim Stern, New York: Central Conference of American Rabbis, and "Siddur Lev Chadash" (1995), edited by Rabbi

Andrew Goldstein, Hertford, United Kingdom: Stephen Austin and Sons, and "Mishkan T'filah" (2007), edited by Rabbi Elyse Frishman, New York: Central Conference of American Rabbis.

"The Torah in Leviticus says 'you shall not be partial'…"

This can be found in Leviticus chapter 19, verse 15. For more on this topic of fairness in justice, please see "Judge Justly, Four Ways," by Lilly Kaufman, Women's League for Conservative Judaism, July 28, 2017, at www.jtsa.edu, or "Beit Din and Judges from the Bible to Modern Times," at www.jewishvirtuallibrary.org

"Reb Zalman on the Standing Prayer…"

This can be found on page 103 of "Jewish with Feeling" by Rabbi Zalman Schachter-Shalomi, New York: Riverhead, 2005.

"The Orthodox view in the Artscroll Siddur…"

This can be found on page 106 of "The Complete Artscroll Siddur," edited by Rabbi Nosson Scherman, Brooklyn: Mesorah Publications, 1994.

"Rabbi Heschel on praying with your feet…"

For more on this topic of prayer as action, please see "Abraham Joshua Heschel" at www.jewishvirtuallibrary.org, or "How Heschel and King Bonded Over the Hebrew Prophets," by Rabbi A. James Rudin, February 11, 2021, at www.religionnews.com or "Following in My Father's Footsteps," by Dr. Susannah Heschel, Vox of Dartmouth, April 4, 2005 at www.dartmouth.edu or "Pray with Your Feet," January 12, 2014, at www.centralsynagogue.org

Chapter Five: What Happens When You Pray for Healing?

"The beautiful mee-sheh-bay-rakh melody of singer-songwriter Debbie Friedman…"

The song that is sung in many congregations is "Mi Shebeirah" by Debbie Friedman, Jewish Music Group, 1995. Or to learn more about this amazing woman who influenced millions of Jews on how to pray with more sincerity, please see "The Feminist Revolution: Debbie Friedman," Jewish Women's Archive, at www.jwa.org, or "Debbie Friedman" at www.reformjudaism.org, or "Debbie Friedman, Singer of Jewish Music," January 11, 2001, www.nytimes. com, or the documentary film "A Journey of Spirit," Ann Coppel Productions, 2015, at www.vimeo.com

"Estimated that more than 85% of Americans pray for healing…"

This refers to a 2016 study by the Gallup organization conducted by Jeff Levin at Baylor University, "Most Americans Pray for Healing," April 28, 2016, at www.baylor.edu, or as described on CNN, April 25, 2016, by Morgan Manella, at www.cnn.com

"There are more than 35,000 prayer circles…"

This can be found at "Many Americans Turn to Prayer for Healing," by Robert Preidt, April 25, 2016, at Health Day, www. cbsnews.com

"At Duke University and several other college and research centers…"

This can be found at "Prayer and Healing," Duke Today, November 30, 2001, or at "Results of First Multicenter Trial of Intercessory Prayer," July 14, 2005, at www.dukehealth.org and "The Healing Power of Prayer?" July 28, 2005 at www.nytimes.com

"Rabbi Amy Eilberg's own words…"

Her essay can be found in "Acts of Loving Kindness: A Training Manual for Bikkur Holim," by Rabbi Nancy Flam, Rabbi Janet Offel, and Rabbi Amy Eilberg, www.studylib.net or in "Jewish Principles of Care for the Dying," by Rabbi Amy Eilberg, "The Outstretched Arm," Winter 2001, at www.jewishboard.org

"In the traditional full version of the Mee Sheh-bay-rakh prayer..."

This can be found on pages 443-444 of "The Complete Artscroll Siddur" by Rabbi Nosson Scherman, Brooklyn: Mesorah Publications, 1994. Or in a shorter version that includes the Debbie Friedman lyrics in "Mishkan T'filah: A Reform Siddur," edited by Rabbi Elyse Frishman, New York: Central Conference of American Rabbis, 2007, pages 109, 371, and 511. This prayer is also discussed in contemporary terms in Chapter Five of "Seven Prayers That Can Change Your Life," by Leonard Felder, Kansas City: Andrews McMeel Publishers, 2001, pages 115-148.

"The last line of the Adon Olam prayer..."

This can be found in most prayer books and is described in "Jewish Prayers: Adon Olam" at www.jewishvirtuallibrary.org

"In the beautiful melodic version by singer-songwriter Craig Taubman..."

This song, B'Yado by Craig Taubman, 1999 and 2014 (Used by Permission) can also be found in several versions on-line as a solo or a duet.

"Rabbi Harold Kushner and others who discuss the randomness and uncertainty..."

This refers to "When Bad Things Happen to Good People," by Rabbi Harold Kushner, New York: Schocken, 1981, and "Saved by Randomness," by Alexander Poltorak, at www.quantumtorah.com and "The Randomness of Life or the Hidden Hand of God," by Rabbi Richard Address, January 14, 2020 at www.jewishsacredaging.com

"B'ezraht HaShem with God's help..."

This can be found in "Jewish Expressions to Start Using Today," by Dr. Yvette Alt Miller, at www.aish.com or in song from Eliana Light at www.jewishlearningmatters.com

Chapter Six: How the Kaddish Works on Many Levels

"Saying the Kaddish to elevate the soul..."

This concept is stated in the Talmud, Sanhedrin 104a. It is explored in "Kaddish Eases Judgment and Elevates the Soul," by Sholom Ber Hecht, at www.chabad.org, and in "Elevating the Soul After Death," at www.mykaddish.com, and in "Shaar Kakavanos" by Rabbi Chaim Vital quoting his teacher Rabbi Isaac Luria, Published by Hotzaas Yerid Haseforim.

"Otis Redding's song..."

The song "I've Been Loving You Too Long to Stop Now" was written by Otis Redding and Jerry Butler, Volt Records, 1965.

"The diverse ways of understanding the word 'soul' in Judaism..."

These are described in "Body and Soul" at www.myjewishlearning.com and in "Glimpses into the Afterlife" by Rabbi Michele Brand Medwin, at www.reformjudaism.org

"Mourning and Mitzvah..."

This book was written by Rabbi Anne Brener, Woodstock, Vermont: Jewish Lights Publishing, 1993, 2001, and 2017.

"Saying Kaddish..."

This book was written by Anita Diamant, New York: Schocken, 1999.

"The Aramaic prayer words are mostly about praising..."

For a history of the Kaddish prayer, please see "Development and History of Kaddish," by Anita Diamant, at www.myjewishlearning.com and "The Origins and Kabbalah of Kaddish," at www.mayimachronim.com

"The research paper at the University of Judaism..."

This refers to "Does a Child Who Has Been Sexually Abused by a Parent Have the Obligation to Say Kaddish for That Parent?" by Benay Lappe, 1993, University of Judaism, at www.avara.org

"Jewish Views of the Afterlife..."

This is a book by Rabbi Simcha Paull Raphael, Lanham, Maryland: Rowman and Littlefield, 1994 and 2019.

"Studies about ADC's: a spontaneous after death communication..."

These studies are summarized and analyzed in "A Systematic Review of Research on After-Death Communication," by Jenny Streit-Horn, PhD, University of North Texas, 2011, at www.digital.library.unt.edu

"The prayer Ayl Mahlay Rakhameem..."

It is described in "El Maleh Rahamim" by Dr. Ronald Eisenberg, at www.myjewishlearning.com and there are different translations found in "Beside Still Waters: A Journey of Comfort and Renewal," compiled by Bayit: Your Jewish Home, Teaneck: New Jersey, Ben Yehuda Press, 2019, pages 61-62.

Chapter Seven: How to Increase the Inner and the Outer Lights

"This compassionate rabbi who would say, "Oy, I don't know what kind of week you had..."

This was Rabbi Ted Falcon, founder of Makom Ohr Shalom in Los Angeles and Bet Alef in Seattle.

"The housewife in 'Fiddler on the Roof' who sang the beautiful Sabbath prayer..."

In the 1971 film version, the role of Golda is played by Norma Crane and the song "Sabbath Prayer" was written by Jerry Bock and Sheldon Harnick.

"A counselor named Nina Amir who has written eBooks and articles on..."

For more information, see www.ninaamir.com/the-priestess-practice or "Create a Sacred Space at Home," by Rahel Musleah at www.rahelsjewishindia.com

"The book 'The Hebrew Priestess...'"

This refers to "The Hebrew Priestess: Ancient and New Visions of Jewish Women's Spiritual Leadership," by Rabbi Jill Hammer and Taya Shere, Teaneck, New Jersey: Ben Yehuda Press, 2015.

"Kabbalistic view of the Sabbath as a preview of a time of harmony and sufficiency..."

In the Talmud, Berachot 57a it describes the Sabbath as "a taste of the world to come." In Rabbi Irving Greenberg's book "The Jewish Way," it describes Shabbat as a taste of a perfect world for a night and a day." For details on how to envision a Shabbat that is a taste of a perfect future, see "Jewish Law, Shabbat and the World to Come," by Rabbi Theodore Friedman, at www.myjewishlearning.com

"The Sabbath as a series of 'spiritual gift certificates'..."

For specifics on how to do this, please see chapter four in "The Ten Challenges" by Leonard Felder, PhD, New York: Crown/Harmony, 1997 and "How I Sustain Myself: Shabbat," by Rabbi Rachel Barenblat, at www.velveteenrabbi.blogs.com and "The Rules of Shabbos," by Rabbi Zalman Schachter-Shalomi, in the book "Jewish with Feeling," New York: Riverhead, 2005, pages 44-49.

"At our congregation the personalized Torah-based theme of the week..."

This refers to the service leader and the musicians inviting a few people to offer a short personal version of the theme from each week's Torah portion at Ahavat Torah Congregation in West Los Angeles, led by Rabbi Miriam Hamrell.

Chapter Eight: What Makes Each Meal More Meaningful?

"The choices of what to say when you are about to take food or drink into your body…"

For more on the different options for prayers over food, please see "Daily Blessings for Food," at www.reformjudaism.org or "Blessings Before Food and Drink," at www.ritualwell.org or "Texts of Blessings Before Eating," at www.chabad.org, or "Blessings in Judaism," by Rabbi Shraga Simmons, at www.aish.com

"A prayer of thanks that our fragile and complicated body works as well as it does…"

This refers to the Asheir Yatzar blessing that is described in Chapter Two and also in the book "Here I Am," by Leonard Felder, New York: Trumpeter, 2011, pages 41-56.

"The body is gently washed and cared for with deep love and respect…"

For more on the practice of "Tahara," washing the body in Judaism before burial, please see Genesis 3:19 and Ecclesiastes 5:14, or "Tahara, Preparing the Body for Burial," at www.myjewishlearning.com or "Preparation for Burial," at www.jewishvirtuallibrary.org

"The body as a holy vessel that houses our soul…"

For more on this Jewish concept, please see "Body and Soul" at www.myjewishlearning.com

"Rabbi Daniel Matt on the prayers of eating…"

His teachings can be found in "The Essential Kabbalah," by Rabbi Daniel Matt, New York: Harper, 1994, page 210.

"At Passover there is a prayer that says, 'Let all who are hungry come and eat'…"

For more on this verse, please see "What Does It Mean to Say 'All Who Are Hungry Come and Eat,'" by Rabbi Elie Kaunfer, at www.myjewishlearning.com and "Let All Who Are Hungry Come and Eat," by Rabbi Andrew Shugerman, at www.jtsa.edu

"The research on Americans who are hungry or food insecure…"

This refers to the 2021 investigation into food insecurity by the Institute for Policy Research at Northwestern University and described in "One in Four Faced Food Insecurity," April 14, 2021, at www.theguardian.com

"The chapter in Leviticus on leaving the gleanings of the harvest for the poor and the stranger…"

This can be found in Leviticus 23:22 and Leviticus 19:9, and is explored in "Gleanings for the Poor," by Dr. Greg Gardner, at www.thetorah.com and in "Gleaning in the Sun," by Emily Landsman, July 28, 2015, at www.jewishfoodexperience.com

"Donating a 10 percent portion…"

This comes from Leviticus chapter 27, verse 30 and Deuteronomy chapter 15, verses 7-8, and is explored in "Tzedakah Basics" at www.aish.com or in "Tzedakah: Charity" by Tracey Rich, at www.jewfaq.org or in "I Always Learned that Jews Give 10 Percent to Charity; Are Other Smaller Percentages OK Too" by Rabbi Tom Alpert, June 25, 2013, at www.jewishboston.com

"Don't close off your own heart…"

For guidance on how to stay open even if there are a lot of people asking you for money, please see "A Code of Jewish Ethics Volume 2: Love Your Neighbor as Yourself," by Rabbi Joseph Telushkin,

New York: Crown/Harmony, 2009, pages 233-242, and "Brother Can You Spare a Dime," by Rabbi Arthur Kurzweil, " at www.dannysiegel.com

"Stewards or guardians of the Earth…"

For more on the Jewish views of taking care of our planet, please see "Genesis and Human Stewardship of the Earth," by Rabbi Yonatan Neril, at www.myjewishlearning.com, or "Judaism and Earth Day," by Rabbi Evan Moffic, at www.reformjudaism.org

"Rabbi Ellen Bernstein and Shomrei Adamah, Keepers of the Earth…"

She is the author of "Ecology and the Jewish Spirit," Woodstock, Vermont: Jewish Lights, 2000 and "The Promised Land: A Passover Haggadah," Milburn, New Jersey: Behrman House, 2020.

"Jewish World Watch and the backpacks for women in war-torn countries…"

For more on their innovative ways to prevent genocide and cruelty, please see "Day 6: Look What You've Done! (the Solar Cooker Project)," at www.jww.org

"Shifra and Puah the midwives in the Passover story…"

This refers to Exodus chapter one, verses 15-21 and is explored in "Puah: Midrash and Aggadah," Jewish Women's Archive, at www.jwa.org, and in "How Two Midwives Tricked Pharaoh," by Hannah Graham Pressman, at www.myjewishlearning.com

Acknowledgements

Many creative and caring individuals guided me on the topics and dilemmas that are explored in this book. Rather than just listing all of their names, I want to focus on a few remarkable souls who taught me that Jewish prayer comes from love, can be taught with love, and can increase the depth of love that we feel and that we express in our daily lives.

Helen Gilbert was a Hebrew School teacher at Temple Israel in Detroit who also was my bar mitzvah tutor when I was twelve years old. Every Monday after school I would meet with her not only to learn the things to memorize but also to talk about real-life issues and personal concerns. She taught me that Jewish educators can be caring, accessible and supportive when kids and teens are going through chaotic and confusing weeks and months. There are hundreds of former students who remember her with great respect and gratitude.

Nancy Shapiro Pikelny has been a consistent friend since we were teenagers in youth group writing creative services for weekend retreats and special events at our temple. She then became an excellent Jewish day-school teacher in Chicago and we've always been able to go right to the truth during our weekly or monthly phone calls all these years. I learned from Nancy that raising Jewish kids and teaching Jewish students are acts of love and connection where the vulnerable human moments are sometimes far more important than the concepts on the syllabus.

Judith Rubenstein is a rabbi's daughter from Connecticut and a friend I met at Kenyon College in Ohio when we were both trying to understand how to stay actively Jewish on a campus that was over 90% non-Jewish in a rural community that was 99% non-Jewish. I learned from Judy that in each decade of life we get challenged to make sure our Judaism stays alive, stays creative, and stays relevant to what's going on inside us and around us.

Debbie Friedman and Craig Taubman are two amazingly talented singer-songwriters who breathed new life into ancient prayers. But equally important is the fact that they were willing to connect one-on-one with kids and adults in such warm ways. Both of these busy people visited at different times the special needs classes that my daughter attended several years ago and they both listened to the questions and concerns of these unique students with complete presence and heartful responses. They taught me that Jewish melodies are not just a "performance," but definitely a way to connect heart to heart.

For three decades, I've been having frequent conversations with my friend Rabbi Marc Sirinsky about all sorts of Jewish dilemmas regarding prayer, activism, family, congregational life, and how to stay balanced and healthy. I am thankful to have a friend who is always growing and endlessly creative.

Rabbi Miriam Hamrell, Rabbi Jackie Redner, Rabbi Ted Falcon, Rabbi Zalman Schachter-Shalomi, Cantorial Soloist Gary Levine, Cantorial Soloist Kimberly Haynes, and many other rabbis and cantors have lifted me up at inspiring services and taught me to breathe, to slow down, to connect, and be fully present during specific Jewish prayers. I am very grateful to be living in a time when Jewish spirituality is not just about heady concepts or arguments, but rather about how to open up our souls and our compassion through the beauty of specific melodies and deeply-meaningful prayer interpretations.

I especially want to thank my beloved wife and best friend Linda Schorin and our courageous, honest daughter Aloni Helen Schorin for teaching me daily what it means to bring caring and openness into every challenging situation and every joyous moment. I am thankful for each day and night when we are able to look into each other's eyes and say, "Thank you to the One who brought us together for so much learning, so many adventures, and so much love."

Most of all, I am grateful to the mysterious Creative Source of Life that guides us and encourages us in so many ways. I hope this book will help many people of all ages to open up and explore their own sense of connecting, feeling distant sometimes, and then re-connecting with the Compassionate Flow and Deep Wisdom that is always present (even when we are not fully aware).

About the Author

Len Felder, PhD is a licensed psychologist and the author of sixteen books on Jewish spirituality and personal growth that have sold over one million copies and were translated into fifteen languages.

His books include "Keeping Your Heart Open," "We See It So Differently," "The Dilemma of the 21st Century Male: Choosing Each Day Between Retro and Forward," "More Fully Alive," "The Ten Challenges," "When a Loved One is Ill," "Here I Am," "Seven Prayers That Can Change Your Life," "Making Peace with Your Parents," "Fitting In Is Overrated," and "When Difficult Relatives Happen to Good People."

Dr. Felder has written for numerous magazines, newspapers, blogs, websites, and research publications, along with appearing on over 150 radio and television programs including "The Today Show on NBC," "Oprah Winfrey," "CNN News," "CBS Morning Show," "National Public Radio," "BBC London," and "Canada A.M."

Active in several volunteer organizations, he received the Distinguished Merit Citation of the National Conference of Christians and Jews for his ten years of co-leading workshops to help teens and adults overcome racism, sexism, homophobia, and religious intolerance.

Originally from Detroit, Dr. Felder graduated with High Honors from Kenyon College in Ohio before working in New York for Doubleday Publishing and later moving to Los Angeles to become a psychologist in private practice.

He and his wife Linda are the parents of Aloni Schorin, a young adult with special needs who writes and co-creates award-winning films and videos on what it's like to be LGBT and Autistic.